Tennessee's
Presidents

Tennessee's Presidents

BY FRANK B. WILLIAMS, JR.

PUBLISHED IN COOPERATION WITH

The Tennessee Historical Commission

THE UNIVERSITY OF TENNESSEE PRESS

KNOXVILLE

TENNESSEE THREE STAR BOOKS / *Paul H. Bergeron, General Editor*

This series of general-interest books about significant Tennessee topics is sponsored jointly by the Tennessee Historical Commission and the University of Tennessee Press.

Cloth: 1st printing, 1981.
Paper: 1st printing, 1981; 2nd printing, 1995.

Library of Congress Cataloging in Publication Data

Williams, Frank Broyles, 1913–
    Tennessee's presidents.
    (Tennessee three star books)
    "Published in cooperation with the Tennessee
    Historical Commission."
    Bibliography: p.
    Includes index.
    1. Presidents—United States—Biography.
2. Jackson, Andrew, 1767–1845. 3. Polk, James K.
(James Knox), 1795–1849. 4. Johnson, Andrew, 1808–
1875. 5. Tennessee—Biography. I. Tennessee
Historical Commission. II. Title. III. Series.
E176.1.W7225   973'.09'92[B]   81-3391
                                     AACR2
ISBN 0-87049-321-3 (cloth: alk. paper)
ISBN 0-87049-322-1 (pbk.: alk. paper)

The paper in this book meets the minimum requirements of the American National Standard for Permanence of Paper for Printed Library Materials. ∞ The binding materials have been chosen for strength and durability.

Cover Photograph: Monument to Three Presidents on Capitol Square, Raleigh, N.C., by Dick Lankford, North Carolina State Archives.

ABOUT THE AUTHOR:

Frank B. Williams, Jr., professor emeritus of history, East Tennessee State University, won that institution's Distinguished Faculty Award in 1977. The author of numerous articles, he was the recipient of the 1955 McClung Award for the best article in *Publications* of the East Tennessee Historical Society.

For Patricia, Ann, and Frank

Preface

In this study of limited scope written for general readers I resorted to eclecticism, re-read a manual on moonshining, fired up my still, and put the doublings through again, again, and again to produce this distillate. In the process I hope that I have not lost the spirits of the subjects or the times in which they lived. For sources I relied primarily on the published letters of Jackson, Polk, and Johnson, and I found, when I read monographs and biographies, that many of the letters I thought important had been used time and again. Perhaps this practice strengthens the belief of Clio's critics that even if history does not repeat itself, historians repeat each other. Historians do not, however, always arrive at the same conclusions. I have tried to produce a brief, readable, and edifying account of Tennessee's three Presidents written primarily from their points of view; I especially tried to portray them as people. Readers wanting more details may find them in the many studies on the Jacksonian period, Manifest Destiny, and Civil War and Reconstruction in addition to the biographies of friends and enemies of the Tennessee triumvirate.

A number of people become involved in the activities of a writer, and I wish to acknowledge the assistance of those who helped me and thank them for their efforts. Friends and acquaintances listened politely as I retold some gems of ribaldry I found in the letters; I appreciate their listening. Richard Harrison Doughty of Greeneville, Tennessee, called my attention to a small item about Johnson's retirement that was reprinted in the *Memphis Commercial Appeal,* May 24, 1972, and graciously permitted the use of photographs from his Johnson Collection. Patricia P. Clark, principal seamstress in the tailor shop managed by LeRoy P. Graf and Ralph W. Haskins, successors to A. Johnson, Tailor, on the campus of the University of Tennessee, graciously supplied some tidbits about the Johnson children. Arthur H. DeRosier, Jr., former president of East Tennessee State University, gave words of encouragement. Head librarians Ed Walters and David Parsely cut some red tape for me. Staff members of the Sherrod Library, East Tennessee State University, ever accommodating and patient, were Polly Creekmore, Edith Keyes, Kathryn Wilson, Dorothy Jones, and Rita Scher. Earl Wade, chairman of the Department of History of East Tennessee State University, in a time of academic penury during the Year of the Crunch, gave me paper clips, notepaper, a feltpoint pen, and a few other goodies from his unreplenishable supplies. Paul Bergeron, editor of the Three Star Books series, demonstrated forebearance when I could not meet deadlines and was most helpful with editorial suggestions. Katherine Holloway, senior editor of U.T. Press, was tactful, skillful, and humorous as she performed painful but necessary editorial chores. Emmett J.B. Essin, my muleborne colleague from Texas, debugged the typescript and polished the prose on several occasions. Burgin E. Dossett, president emeritus of East Tennessee State University, read the typescript and made valuable suggestions for its improvement. My colleague Eric R. Lacy shared his knowledge of Tennessee history with me and read the typescript. If the standards of the Clioian guild permitted, I would disown errors discovered hereinafter and assign them to my editor and readers. Alas, we do not operate that way, so I acknowledge responsibility for them. Katie, my bride of four decades, provided not only encouragement but a corner of the den in Bankrupt Court Manor where I worked and which she seldom cleared of clutter; she kept me supplied with limes which I used as antiscorbutics. Without complaint she permitted me to postpone a number of chores she had saved for several years in anticipation of my retirement. To Katie and the other folks, thanks.

February 7, 1981   FRANK B. WILLIAMS, JR.

Contents

ILLUSTRATIONS

Tennessee's Presidents

1. The Milieu of the Triumvirate

In a period of thirty-eight years, two young men and a boy moved from North Carolina to Tennessee. Andrew Jackson arrived in 1788 when the territory was the frontier and Nashville was the cutting edge; he had a license to practice law; he had his pistols, a horse or two, and a few dogs, and in his saddle bags were his clothes and maybe two or three lawbooks. In 1806, James K. Polk traveled with his parents encumbered with wagons of furniture, some slaves, and livestock; they settled on a farm in Maury County. Andrew Johnson and three relatives crossed the same mountains with their few belongings in a small horse-drawn wagon; he hung out his tailor's sign in Greeneville in 1826. With the passing years each man in his own way cut a path through the tangle of state politics that bisected the road to the White House. Their age differences and relations were such that Polk came to be regarded as Jackson's protégé. Johnson, as a young legislator, sometimes visited Jackson's Hermitage in the company of others to pay homage to the retired leader. Congressman Johnson and President Polk agreed on major issues but each considered the other his personal enemy.

Early settlers, especially businessmen and politicians, as in other western states of the time, did not let contemporary transportation facilities interfere with their mobility. Jackson, for example, in the 1790s, rode horseback to Philadelphia, purchased goods for his store, shipped them overland to Pittsburgh, and floated them in keelboats and flatboats down the Ohio and up the Cumberland rivers. New Orleans was the port of exit for goods from Tennessee. East Tennesseans transported supplies from Philadelphia in conestoga wagons. In 1804, the road from Nashville to Washington crossed the Cumberland Plateau to Crab Orchard and ran northeast through Knoxville, Jonesborough, Abingdon, Lexington, Staunton, Winchester, Orange Court House, and Fairfax Court House. Steamboating on the Cumberland began in March 1819, when *General Jackson* ran out her gangplank at the Nashville landing. Such were the comforts of the boats that Jackson in 1829 and Polk in 1845, although experienced and hardy overland travelers, chose to begin their inaugural journeys riding on the water. Having retired as President, Jackson began his homeward trip in 1837 with a ride in the steam cars and then changed to coach and steamboat. Polk utilized trains, boats, and carriages when he returned to Nashville in 1849. Johnson used stagecoaches in his early trips to Washington and trains in the later days.

Traveling by boat and train involved risks of derailing, boiler explosions, collisions, and sinkings. Fear of cholera on the river forced travelers into bone-rattling stagecoaches that were subject to upsets, turning over in flooded streams, and broken axles. Some fellow passengers were obnoxious; the food and accommodations at coach stops in many cases were inferior. Senator Hopkins L. Turney, returning home in 1838, survived a sinking and a coach wreck and described his journey as "tiresome." In 1857, Johnson suffered a dislocated elbow and a crushed arm in a railroad accident.

Communications improved with the passing of time. In 1832, one of Polk's correspondents in Fayetteville, Tennessee, commented on receiving a letter from Washington in seventeen days. On the eve of the Civil War, Senator Johnson received a letter from home twenty-six hours after it was mailed — thanks to the railroads. (The postal service would be hard pressed to duplicate this feat 120 years later.) President Polk marveled at the use of the "magnetic telegraph"; not many years thereafter Military Governor Johnson raised unshirted hell with an impertinent captain who questioned his excessive telegraphic bills.

Among the issues that agitated the public mind in the first half of the nineteenth century was public schools. Not many political leaders in Tennessee expressed serious concern about a state-supported system of education. Literate parents on the frontier taught their children to read and write. If they were financially able, and many could afford the nominal fees, they patronized private academies where their offspring learned the fundamentals of a classical education. Of the presidents-to-be perhaps Johnson, who had no formal schooling, was the logical one to speak out for state schools. During his first term as governor, in the 1850s, he called for new taxes to support elementary schools, and the legislature responded.

Like people in other western states, Tennesseans were interested in higher education, and they incorporated a number of colleges in the days of Jackson, Polk, and Johnson. Several deserve some attention. Greeneville College, chartered by the territorial legislature in 1794, opened in 1802. Johnson, the young tailor, became friendly with members of its literary and debating societies; in their clubrooms he learned the fundamentals of formal argument if not persuasion. Blount College in Knoxville, chartered in 1794, survived difficult times to become East Tennessee University in 1840 and the University of Tennessee in 1879. The University of Nashville (1826) evolved from an academy opened in 1785 and Cumberland College that was organized in 1806; with its department of medicine the University of Nashville became the best school in the state in the antebellum period. Jackson enrolled his ward and his son in the university. Polk permitted his brother William to register there after he dropped out of the University of North Carolina; other relatives Polk sent to Yale. Cumberland Presbyterians organized and supported Cumberland University in Lebanon in 1842; graduates of its law department made the institution well known. A number of other colleges were organized during the period, but not all deserved the label of an institution of higher learning. Many people, however, thought in terms of quantity rather than quality, and their attitude may have been voiced by an egocentric Nashvillian who boasted of the nine colleges within a fifty-mile radius that he equated with Harvard. Of the triumvirate only Polk received a college education.

Another issue that Governors Polk and Johnson faced was that of prison reform. Neither gave much attention to it. Polk did recommend that suitable quarters be provided female convicts in the penitentiary and asked the legislature to amend the criminal laws so the governor could commute death sentences without giving full pardons to prisoners; he approved the practice of reducing terms for good behavior. Johnson strongly condemned the idea that criminals could be reformed; teaching prisoners a trade was heinous because freed felons competed with honest mechanics. He earnestly appealed to the legislature for changes in the law so respectable citizens would be protected from such degrading competition.

Three other reform movements gave little trouble to the triumvirate. Such was the climate of opinion in Tennessee in the 1850s that Johnson and his opponent in the gubernatorial race hardly noticed the petition of the temperance union. Neither women's rights nor labor unions excited them. Johnson as alderman, legislator, congressman, governor, senator, and President always reminded his audiences of his humble beginnings as a mechanic and claimed that he spoke for all working classes.

Under the influence of Jeffersonian republicanism that led to Jacksonian democracy, the states broadened the electorate by abolishing prop-

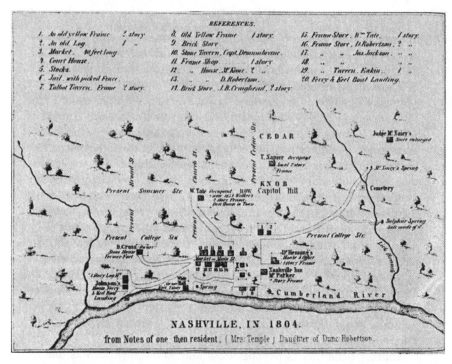

REFERENCES.

1. An old yellow Frame   2 story.
2. An old Log   1 ..
3. Market   40 feet long.
4. Court House.
5. Stocks.
6. Jail, with picked Fence.
7. Talbot Tavern. Frame 2 story.

8. Old Yellow Frame   1 story.
9. Brick Store.
10. Stone Tavern, Capt. Demumbrane.
11. Frame Shop   1 story.
12. .. House, McKine   2 ..
13. .. .. D. Robertson.
14. Brick Store. J.B. Craighead, 2 story.

15. Frame Store, Wm Tate.   1 story.
16. Frame Store, D. Robertson.   2 ..
17. .. .. Jas Jackson   ..
18. .. ..
19. Tavern. Eakin   1 ..
20. Ferry & Keel Boat Landing.

NASHVILLE, IN 1804.

from Notes of one then resident. (Mrs. Temple j Daughter of Dunc Robertson.

STATE CAPITOL, NASHVILLE, TENNESSEE.

erty requirements and launched the so-called era of the common man. Jackson rode the crest of the wave into the White House, although in 1828 he hardly qualified as a commoner; he was, however, the hero of the masses. Polk paid lip service to Jacksonian democracy when he took to the hustings. Johnson made the most of his opportunities and never let the voters forget that he was the working men's working man.

Of all the reform movements the abolition of slavery attracted the most attention. The three Tennesseans were slaveowners. Growing up and living in the south, they accepted slavery as part of their environment and believed that slavery had the sanction of God. They believed that the Founding Fathers in their wisdom protected the institution when they wrote the guarantees of property rights into the fundamental law. The Tennesseans also accepted the compromises on slavery as they were made. Jackson and Polk deplored abolitionists' attempts to associate slavery with territorial expansion. All three feared the crisis which they realized was developing. Jackson and Polk were not around when the war started, but Johnson wished for a Jackson in the White House as he damned abolitionists and seceding southern aristocrats as he defined the word — with equal fervor.

In 1860, the population of Tennessee had grown to 1,109,801. Memphis was the largest city with 22,621 inhabitants, and Nashville ranked second in size with 16,988. Knoxville had 5,300, while in the southeastern corner of the state 2,545 people lived in Chattanooga. Most Tennesseans were yeomen who earned their living on farms that produced corn, cotton, tobacco, and wheat as major crops, and where they raised cattle, sheep, horses, mules, and hogs. The agricultural economy was dominant, but some manufacturing was done in relatively small shops. Textile mills, incidentally, did not do well in the state. Iron mines supported many small bloomeries, foundries, and furnaces; and coal and copper mines were developed before the war. Many small water-powered mills dotted the countryside and supplied the people with flour and cornmeal.

Tennesseans did have opportunities for self-improvement and recreation. Printers' supplies were comparatively cheap, politicians needed publicity, and a number of men fancied themselves as writers. Many

---

(*Above*): Nashville map reflecting some of the growth of that town at the time of Jackson's early career as a lawyer and influential citizen. (*Below*): An early sketch of the state capitol building in Nashville. Illustrations from A.W. Putnam, *History of Middle Tennessee.*

newspapers were started, and a few of them flourished. Before the telegraph was installed, editors copied national and European news from
eastern and New Orleans papers, distorted local and state news, and lied
outrageously about their political enemies while blatantly exaggerating
the virtues of their party-backers. Traveling thespians — Ole Bull, Jenny
Lind, Edwin Booth, and others — took culture to the river towns of
Nashville and Memphis where society belles and dames could glitter and
twitter. Meanwhile in the villages, on the farms, and in the cabins, pro-
genitors of Grand Ole Opry stars and preservers of Appalachian culture
used gut and horsehair to produce foot-stomping rhythms. Ballad sing-
ers kept alive the stories of unrequited love, unfaithful spouses, the cer-
tainty of death, and life thereafter. Muster days for the militia, political
rallies, and camp-meetings of Methodists and Baptists brought surcease
from drudgery to the country folk; the brawls, mayhem, homicides,
feuds, and bastards that resulted from the gatherings gave the people
something to talk about for months.

Such were the times of Jackson, Polk, and Johnson. The environment, the issues, and the people did influence each man in his rise to
power. None of the three considered himself as a reformer, but each man
made decisions that had lasting effects on the country.

2. Tennessee's First President, Imperious Andrew

On May 12, 1788, in the little log courthouse in the frontier village of Jonesborough, Western District of North Carolina (later Tennessee) Andrew Jackson, twenty-one years old, presented his credentials to the presiding judge and received permission to practice law in the district that extended 300 miles westward to the Cumberland settlements. Before he died fifty-seven years later, Jackson served his adopted state as judge, militia general, congressman, and United States senator; he served his country as a victorious general, a territorial governor, and President. In the process he acquired worldly goods to qualify as a lord of a manor. All of these achievements did much to compensate for his youthful inferiority complex, if, indeed, they did not result in the feeling of superiority.

Jackson, born in the Waxhaw settlements on the border of North and South Carolina, claimed the latter as his native state. Andy's father died before he was born, and his mother and brothers died during the Revolutionary War, so he was reared by relatives. He attended a local academy and learned the fundamentals, but he was not a bookish lad. Late in 1782, he came into a small inheritance and headed for Charleston where he learned some of the manners of the gentry as he wenched, gambled, and drank with sporty youngbloods. What a beginning for a fifteen-year-old boy! Out of funds he returned to Waxhaw, briefly resumed his education, and then taught for a term or two in a community school.

The study and practice of law provided young men with many opportunities for advancement in the late eighteenth century. As befitted a young man on the make, Jackson decided to "read law" and worked out an agreement with Spruce McCay of Salisbury, a competent lawyer with an adequate library. From 1784 to 1786, Jackson served his apprenticeship in company of John McNairy and several other men. In the process of learning enough law to meet his needs in the frontier courts, Andy supported himself by betting on horseraces and playing cards; he also polished his manners, courted the girls, attended dancing school, and

played practical jokes. As a manager of the Christmas ball, Jackson arranged for the town whores, a mother-and-daughter team, to attend;
the nice people in town talked about the outrage for years afterward.
After passing his bar examinations the young attorney rode the circuit
without attracting a clientele. McNairy, appointed judge of the Superior
Court for the Western District of North Carolina, offered Jackson the
position of public prosecutor. They crossed the mountains in the spring
and began their labors on that day in May 1788. Jackson tried a few
cases, indulged in horseracing, displayed what he considered the manners of a gentleman, and laid the foundations for a reputation as a duelist when he challenged Waightstill Avery for insulting (really hazing)
him in court.

Public Prosecutor Jackson and Judge McNairy waited until fall to begin their journey to Nashville. Traveling in a company of some 100 settlers and narrowly escaping from Indians, they arrived to discover a few
hundred inhabitants living in houses, cabins, and tents in the town that
could boast of two stores, two taverns, a courthouse, and a distillery.
Some 5,000 other settlers lived in stations along the Cumberland River.
These were litigious people whose disputes over land titles, debts, and
contracts kept Jackson, who could engage in civil practice, busy. He
dealt with horsethieves, rapists, murderers, perjurers, and petty criminals. As a prosecutor he secured convictions in 62 percent of his cases.
He was involved in more than 400 civil cases between 1788 and 1798, the
second largest practice among sixteen attorneys in Nashville. Although
doing most of his legal work in Nashville, Jackson rode the circuit that
extended to Knoxville and Jonesborough; he crossed the Cumberland
Plateau twenty-two times in a seven-year period. Clearly, Jackson was
more than a "poor, pitiful, pettyfogging lawyer." Legal fees were regu-
lated in those days, so Jackson's income came primarily from the volume of business; he received about $600 per year as prosecutor. Jackson,
as did many other shrewd men on the frontier, also learned how to spec-
ulate in land.

Several months after his arrival in Nashville, Jackson sought lodging
in the compound of Mrs. John Donelson, widow of one of the founders
of the settlement and matriarch of the large Donelson clan whose children and in-laws were prominent leaders. Jackson's choice of a boarding
house had profound influence on his career. For one thing, he shared a
cabin with John Overton, a young lawyer, who became a life-long friend,
confidant, counselor, and, on occasion, business partner. More important, he met Rachel Donelson Robards, his landlady's daughter. Rachel,

a comely, vivacious brunette, was unhappily married to Lewis Robards, an insanely jealous and unfaithful husband; their marital troubles had resulted in one separation and reconciliation. According to most accounts, Andy's attentions to Rachel were proper, but Robards became suspicious and created a scene. Overton persuaded Jackson to move as a matter of propriety. Robards returned to his home in Kentucky; soon Rachel heard that he intended to come for her. Frightened, she decided to visit friends in Spanish Natchez, and Jackson either volunteered or was requested to go along as a protector. If they were not already in love, Rachel and Andrew had become warm friends, and he visited her several times between January 1790 and March 1791. Robards talked about Rachel's elopement with another man and petitioned the legislature of Virginia for a divorce. Early in 1791, Nashvillians heard that the legislature had passed an enabling act which permitted the aggrieved husband to sue, but they misinterpreted the action and assumed that it had granted a divorce as was the practice in Tennessee and North Carolina. Jackson hastened to Natchez where he and Rachel were married. Robards gave the couple plenty of time to prove his charge of adultery and did not get the final decree until September 1793.

The Nashville gentry accepted Rachel and Andrew. After all, the Donelsons were prominent and well-to-do people by frontier standards, and Jackson was a promising young lawyer who had come to the notice of Territorial Governor William Blount. Friends and neighbors took the embarrassment of a second marriage in stride. Gossips kept their voices lowered if they mentioned it at all because the young attorney's quick temper, marksmanship, and concept of personal honor discouraged loose talk in the places where men congregated. John Sevier was one of the first to mention the unfortunate circumstances publicly when he and Jackson exchanged insults in Knoxville in 1803. That led to a challenge and the famous and farcial pistol-and-cutlass show on the Kingston road. Fortunately, no bloodshed resulted; only the dignity of the judge and governor suffered. Over thirty years after the marriage when Jackson was a presidential candidate, his political enemies provided exaggerated and distorted versions and lies for the opposition press whose reporters would be called "investigative" in the late twentieth century.

Rachel Jackson, in 1791, was a woman of the frontier and that she remained all of her life. She was not well educated, as her letters show, but she had a good mind and more than her share of common sense. She and Andrew were devoted to each other. She bewailed his many long absences from home as she told him about the farm and the cute sayings of their adopted son, Andrew Junior. Jackson worried about Rachel and requested a relative to keep her cheerful because her tears "fills me with woe." In his letters he advised her on farm management and business matters. Rachel, for her part, conducted a profitable operation. After she died and Jackson became President, his overseers and son lost money at the Hermitage.

Although Rachel and Andrew had no children of their own, their homes were filled with her nieces and nephews. The general served as guardian for children of several deceased friends, and the children returned the love and affection lavished on them. Jackson gave Cupid a helping hand when he encouraged Andrew Jackson Hutchings, a ward, to marry Mary Coffee, daughter of his deceased friend, John Coffee. Hutchings, he told Mary, would be an affectionate and industrious husband. He advised Hutchings to marry a woman who worked hard and saved money, and he cited Rachel as a model helpmate who had saved him from ruin. After the couple married, Jackson confided to the young husband, "Good humor is the weapon that keeps a wife affectionate and true."

On December 22, 1809, Sevren and Elizabeth Donelson became the parents of twins. Elizabeth could not care for both boys, so Rachel took one of her nephews home. She and Andrew became fond of the infant and adopted him. They spoiled him, and by the time Jackson became President, Andrew Junior had the marks of a gentleman — expensive tastes, polished manners, a gracious host, and a way with women. While visiting in Philadelphia, Andrew Junior met and fell in love with Sarah Yorke. They were married in November 1831. Sarah met all of the President's qualifications for a daughter-in-law, and he loved her deeply; Sarah reciprocated his affection. In time the President became a fond grandfather and exercised his right to spoil his grandchildren. Jackson turned the management of the Hermitage over to Junior who never mastered profitable farm practices. Friends and acquaintances took advantage of him, crops failed, and his drinking habits embarrassed his family. Andrew Junior probably did the best he could, but indebtedness became a way of life and insolvency his fate.

Jackson, with his almost maniacal urge to succeed, became involved in a number of business ventures that included land speculation, merchandising, distilling, slave trading, and having a boatyard and a cotton gin. Like many of his contemporaries on the Tennessee frontier and as a protégé of William Blount, Jackson became an adept land speculator whose activities dovetailed nicely with his law practice. He had a profitable partnership with John Overton on the banks of the Mississippi River from which Memphis evolved. As a congressman in 1798, his ethics did not preclude his using inside information to tell Robert Hays that a treaty with the Cherokees would soon open land on the Duck River. "This is as much as to say to you," he wrote, "to keep all you have and get what you can." Jackson bought land in West Tennessee, Mississippi, and Alabama. When short of cash in later years, he usually had a parcel of land he could sell.

As a farmer, Jackson eschewed the more pretentious classification of "planter" and relied primarily on his comparatively small holdings first at Poplar Grove, then Hunter's Hill, and later the Hermitage where, in 1812, he tilled 640 acres. He and Andrew Junior bought Halcyon Plantation in Mississippi that included some 1100 acres after he retired from the presidency. Jackson owned twenty slaves in 1812 and about 150 in 1842. The Hermitage, Jackson thought, not only should be profitable but self-sufficient. He raised sheep for wool and swine for meat; shoes and clothing for his people were made on the place. During his presidency Jackson received detailed reports from his overseers and his son on the condition of crops and slaves; even "Littleton's" case of "gonerea, he got . . . from his wife" did not go unnoticed. Jackson, a connoisseur of horseflesh since childhood and befitting a man who hankered for patrician status, bought, raised, sold, trained, and bet on thoroughbreds. His famed "Truxton" won sizeable bets, brought in many stud fees, and contributed to the bad feelings that resulted in the Dickinson duel. Farmer Jackson's most profitable years were from 1805 to 1819 when he was comparatively close to home, before he contracted his acute case of presidential itch, when growing seasons were favorable, and when cotton generally sold for a good price.

Political leaders like to have intelligent, ambitious, loyal, and dependable young men in their organizations. William Blount, governor of the Territory South of the River Ohio, was a wily politician and as skillful a land pirate as graced the frontier. The young prosecutor and lawyer in Nashville attracted his attention. Blount appointed him attorney general in the Mero district in 1791. The next year, Lawyer Jackson, without military training, became judge advocate in a cavalry regiment in Davidson County. After all, service in the militia was a good way to meet many people. Tennesseans, led by Blount, moved toward statehood in 1796, and Jackson served as a delegate to the constitutional convention. As a western man Jackson hated Indians and their backers, Spaniards and Britishers, who stood in the way of cheap lands and western expansion. Like most other Tennesseans he favored the Jeffersonian Republicans. Blount could use a man like Jackson, and Jackson probably learned valuable political lessons as he observed the governor in action.

Jackson, with Blount's support, was elected as the state's sole congressman, and he soon replaced Blount in the Senate after the latter's intrigues forced him out. Jackson did not distinguish himself in Congress and made an unfavorable impression on Thomas Jefferson who presided over the Senate. The Tennessean did, however, oppose payment of bribes to Barbary pirates, did vote funds for new frigates, and did protest the Federalists' attitude toward Indians and Great Britain. Perhaps the young politician had gone beyond his depth because he wrote Overton about his "disquietude in political life" and assured him that his political career would be brief. He resigned in June 1798.

Soon after returning home, Jackson was appointed to the state supreme court. The position paid $600 a year, which the judge could use. It also afforded him an opportunity to strengthen his political base as he rode the circuit from Nashville to Jonesborough. For six years Jackson rendered fair and "generally right" decisions, although none displayed profound scholarship. While maintaining judicial decorum on the bench, he also was capable of adjourning court as he did in Jonesborough and becoming a one-man posse to round up the recalcitrant Russell Bean who had cowed not only the townspeople but also the sheriff and his deputies.

Ambitious and talented young men in the early days of the republic knew that one path to financial and political success was military service, and they had ample opportunity, if not the necessity, to serve. Retreating Indians on the advancing frontier received aid and encouragement from English and Spanish agents whose home governments correctly considered the United States as threat to their adjacent empires. In 1796, John Sevier became governor and resigned as major general commanding the militia. The brash Andrew, without real military experience, became a candidate for the post that was filled by a vote of field grade officers. Sevier had another man in mind, so Jackson lost. In 1802, the command became vacant again, and Jackson, still lusting for military office — it would not conflict with judicial duties — became a candidate. This time he was prepared because he had courted militia officers and won friends as he rode his circuit. Sevier, having recently finished his first series of three terms as governor, wanted the job. The field officers voted 17 to 17, and Governor Archibald Roane broke the tie by supporting Jackson whom he regarded as the leader of the Blount faction in Nashville. This affected the egos of both candidates, and it certainly had an impact on politics in Tennessee.

Major General Jackson had comparatively peaceful times in which to familiarize himself with the paper work involving his command while he looked after his farm and other interests. In May 1805, he also became involved in the intrigues of Aaron Burr who was made welcome by Nash-villians and entertained at the Hermitage. Burr apparently led Jackson to believe that he had designs on the Spanish Southwest and the secretary of war approved the plans; Burr also bought supplies and flatboats from the enterprising general. Some time later Jackson heard that Burr and General James Wilkinson, who commanded troops in Louisiana, planned to take New Orleans. Thinking that he detected signs of treason, Jackson warned Governor William C.C. Claiborne of Louisiana and President Jefferson.

After Burr was arrested in Natchez and returned to Richmond for trial, Jackson received a summons to appear as a witness. Convinced that Burr had no treasonable intentions, the general regarded the trial as nothing less than "political persecution." He proclaimed his belief from street level and barroom floors if not from the housetops, so he was never called to testify. Wilkinson, Jackson believed, was capable of treachery because he was in the pay of Spain. Jackson showed bad judgment in his involvement with Burr, but he learned (according to Robert V. Remini) that western expansion could succeed only when backed by the authority of the government.

While relations with the warring European countries plagued President James Madison, Jackson decided that the United States would have to take a stand against Britain. Accordingly, he ordered company commanders to have fortnightly drills and discipline their troops in preparation for the clash of arms. After the declaration of war in June 1812, Jackson waited for orders that he feared would place him and his Tennesseans under the command of "General Don James Wilkinson."

Jackson's forebodings soon became facts of life. He assembled 2,000 troops and supplies and in late December proceeded to the "lower Countrys"; he sent mounted troops over land to Natchez, and he accompanied the infantry on the torturous trip in flatboats down the Cumberland, Ohio, and Mississipi rivers. Jackson kept Wilkinson informed of his progress, and the two were warily polite in their correspondence. Receiving no assignment after reaching Natchez, Jackson bewailed inactivity because "Indolence creates disquiet" among troops. He struggled with logistical problems and bombarded Wilkinson and Secretary of

War John Armstrong with demands for supplies. In the middle of March, Jackson received orders to discharge his men without pay and turn all government property over to Wilkinson; planners in Washington no longer considered New Orleans threatened. With their commander declaring that his troops "followed me into the field" and "I shall carefully march them back to their homes," the Tennesseans began their homeward trek.

Short of supplies, Jackson had to use his personal credit to buy medicine for his ailing soldiers. When there was no longer room for all of the sick in the wagons, the officers turned their horses over to those strong enough to ride; the general himself declared that he walked all the way from Natchez to Nashville except for some twenty miles. The Natchez campaign, if campaign it was, brought out the best qualities of the commander. He endeared himself to his men by sharing and trying to alleviate their miseries. He displayed will power and determination to triumph over adversity. Without qualms he took on the brass in the paper war and probably enjoyed a glow of satisfaction as he composed his letters of protest.

During the summer of 1813, the general enjoyed the plaudits of the public and went about his business with the homefolks. He became involved in a dispute with Jesse and Thomas Hart Benton that resulted in the shoot-out in the City Hotel in Nashville and left Jackson with a shattered left shoulder, a broken arm, and near death from loss of blood. While he recuperated, news came of the Creek massacre at Fort Mims in Alabama. Governor Willie Blount called out the militia, and the general left his bed to lead his troops in his second campaign of the War of 1812.

Jackson, land hungry and expansionist westerner that he was, began his campaign with a definite goal in mind. He intended to crush the Indians, cut a road to Mobile, and conquer Spanish Florida, the source of Creek supplies. Myopic authorities in Washington had other ideas. With General Thomas Pinckney in overall command, troops from Mississippi and Georgia were supposed to advance on the flanks while Tennesseans pushed southward. As the campaign developed, the Georgians and Mississippians faltered, General John Cocke with his East Tennesseans arrived late, and Jackson's troops bore the brunt of the fighting.

Aggressive in war as he was in private life, Jackson became impatient when civilian contractors failed to deliver supplies, and he rapidly pushed deep into Alabama without them. His men defeated the Red Sticks (the warring faction of the Creek Nation) on November 3 and 9, 1813, but lack of supplies prevented Jackson from following up his victories. At

Fort Strother the little army all but starved, and the general, not recovered from his wounds and stricken with dysentery, shared his acorns with a hungry private. While he angrily wrote letters to his superiors, Jackson faced "turbulent and mutinous" men in camp. Combined with the problems from winter weather, inadequate clothing, and starvation was the argument between commander and troops over the terms of their enlistment. On three occasions the volunteers started for home only to turn back in the face of Jackson's curses, a few cavalrymen, loaded cannon, and a musket which the general later discovered was inoperable. Governor Blount and the secretary of war agreed with the soldiers that their tour ended in December and advised Jackson to return home. "Retrograde" he would not; he chose to remain at Fort Strother with 130 men while he appealed to Blount to call up 5,000 new troops and pointed out that all of the frontier lay at the mercy of the Creeks and their European allies. This was his nadir.

Better days were ahead. Blount changed his mind and called up more troops. In March 1814, Jackson had almost 5,000 men, and with advanced posts established and his supply base well guarded, he was ready to move. First, however, he had the unpleasant duty of executing Private John Woods who had been court martialed and found guilty of disobedience, disrespect, and mutiny. Pardoned once for the same offenses, Woods had not mended his ways. Jackson upheld the sentence and made an example of Woods. During the presidential campaign of 1828, political enemies figuratively exhumed the skeletons of Woods and others in an attempt to damn the old hero. No American general has had to deal with such widespread mutiny as Jackson, and his decision had a salutary effect on his men. The public execution over, the general marched his troops to Horseshoe Bend and decisively defeated the Red Sticks. The battle eliminated the "Indian menace" in the Old Southwest and partially satisfied the appetite for land. General Pinckney arrived to relieve Jackson and his Tennesseans, who then went home to be welcomed as heroes. Victory on any field has a way of silencing the voices and dulling the memories of mutinous soldiers, carping politicians, personal enemies, and a fickle public. The general was the greatest hero, and even that portion of Nashville nabobs who considered him a brawler and duelist kept quiet.

Jackson's exploits in the Old Southwest had to be recognized by authorities in Washington who had few victories to sustain them as one disaster followed another in other sections of the country and as blue-light Yankees in New England trafficked with the enemy and talked about se-

cession. In Jackson the people had a hardheaded general unafraid of writing bluntly to superiors, who surmounted adversity, took the war to the enemy, and won. His men had confidence in him and followed him. Jackson, with some disappointment, accepted a commission as a brigadier general in the regular army; politics, however, soon resulted in a vacancy among the ranks of major generals, so he attained one of his long-sought goals. He commanded a military district.

Major General Jackson began his third campaign in mid-summer when he returned to Alabama and forced the terms of the Treaty of Fort Jackson on Creek chiefs. He moved on to fortify Mobile, which, he correctly guessed, the British planned to use as a base for supplying the Indians and conquering the Gulf Coast. After turning back a British attempt to enter Mobile Bay in September, the general on his own responsibility — an earlier request had been denied by his superiors — marched his men to Pensacola and forced the British to withdraw. Warned by his spies — from Washington came a similar message — that a huge British expedition prepared to sail from Jamaica to New Orleans, Jackson returned to Mobile, arranged for the defense of his eastern flank, and moved to the Crescent City.

Arriving in New Orleans on December 1, Jackson found the citizens confused and frightened. With the help of his friend Edward Livingston, he charmed the ladies with his suave and courtly manners — they expected a barbarian — and bolstered the morale of the local military companies and civilians with reviews and parades. The general caused the natives to raise their eyebrows when he accepted the services of a company of free Negroes and Jean Lafitte's "hellish banditti" who were experienced cannoneers. Some of the businessmen were disturbed by his feverish preparations and imposition of martial law. Jackson urged commanders of troops from Kentucky, Mississippi, and Tennessee to hurry forward while he ordered outposts placed on all approaches to the city.

On December 13, the British ships entered Lake Borgne, and scouting parties slowly probed the bayous and swamps for an unguarded path. A popular military aphorism is that in every operation "one poor son of a bitch never gets the word." (According to tradition, the saying began during the Revolutionary War when John Paul Jones was called upon to

A Currier print of Jackson done sometime shortly after his death in 1845. Courtesy of Special Collections, University of Tennessee Library.

surrender, and he replied, "I have just begun to fight." A man in the crow's nest heard him, surveyed the carnage and gore on the deck below, and muttered, "There is always one poor son of a bitch who never gets the word.") Some incompetent American of dubious ancestry had not manned the Bayou Bienvenu; the British found it and went ashore in force. The struggle for New Orleans began on the night of December 23 and ended January 8, 1815. Jackson's reinforcements arrived in time, and from behind their fortifications his "Dirty Shirts" from Tennessee who could "bark" a squirrel at a hundred yards used their skills to turn back assault after assault. (To bark a squirrel the rifleman shoots by the side of the squirrel's head; the concussion or the fall kills the squirrel. Thus the animal is unblooded; some epicureans insist that death by barking improves the taste of squirrels.)

Jackson won the battle but not the war because American and British commissioners had agreed on peace terms in Ghent on December 24, 1814. Had the British captured New Orleans and established an occupation government they could have re-opened negotiations, on the basis of right of possession, and taken Louisiana or returned it to Spain. For two months after the battle Jackson held the city under martial law while some of the citizens called him tyrannical and ceased to regard him as a savior. When he received official notification of the war's end, the general immediately restored civil government and wound up his affairs, but not before federal Judge Dominick Hall fined him for contempt of court. He returned to Nashville for receptions befitting a hero—and in time for the summer races.

From the Hermitage, Jackson commanded his district and seemed content to live the life of a country gentleman. Farm commodities brought good prices, and with his salary and allowances he was comfortable if not affluent. The general journeyed to Washington in the fall of 1815, and people turned out to greet and fete him. Even the sage of Monticello descended his mountain to exchange toasts in Lynchburg. Returning home in the spring, Jackson watched over negotiations with Indian tribes, indulged his penchant for epistolary controversy, and thought of East Florida.

Troubles with the Seminoles worsened, and Jackson received orders late in 1817 to take personal command of the troops. He could, if necessary, enter Spanish territory in pursuit of Indians. President James Monroe and the general understood each other's longing for Florida; the latter did ask for authority to seize the territory on the ground that it was used as a base by Indians and others to launch attacks. Jackson suggested that the President's wishes could be conveyed through Tennessee Congressman John Rhea. The general never received a direct answer, although he always argued that he had and he destroyed the letter. Anyway, his directives were sufficiently (intentionally?) vague for his broad interpretation, so he set out for Seminole country and pushed into the Spanish territory with the excuse that the officials could not control the Indians—it was a matter of self defense. In the course of fighting the Indians on Spanish soil, Jackson captured two British subjects, Robert Ambrister and Alexander Arbuthnot, whom he accused of aiding the enemy. Both were tried and executed. Leaving part of his army around St. Marks, Jackson turned westward to Pensacola where he believed Indians had taken refuge. He took the town and the weakly-held fort, received the surrender of the governor, and claimed that Florida was under American control. The war against the Indians, Jackson wrote Monroe, was ended; if his health improved and with a few reinforcements he could take Cuba. Neither of these conditions was fulfilled, and Jackson went home.

Monroe and his cabinet had to face the protests of the British and Spanish governments while the general regained his strength and enjoyed the ego massage by an admiring public and press—he and his contemporaries did not live in an age when they had to apologize for defending what they considered their nation's interests. The president was in a position where he could neither withdraw from Florida nor censure Jackson. In the cabinet discussions only John Quincy Adams, secretary of state, defended the hero because he could use the affair as a position of strength from which to negotiate a settlement of the western boundaries with Spain and nudge her into selling Florida. This he did in the Adams-Onis Treaty of 1819. Jackson, on the other hand, thought that Adams was critical of his action and for years believed that Secretary of War John C. Calhoun had defended him.

Speaker of the House Henry Clay and William H. Crawford, secretary of treasury—both of whom had presidential ambitions—began to think of Jackson as a competitor. The hero, they decided, should be eliminated before he grew too strong. Clay and Crawford's congressional friends introduced resolutions censuring Jackson and calling for laws to restrain impulsive generals in the future. Jackson hastened to Washington where he aided Senator John H. Eaton, Representative Felix Grundy, and others in preparing his defense. Clay's eloquence won few votes, and the resolutions met decisive defeat. A critical committee report in the Senate never came to a vote, but the general's temper boiled over. Jackson, after the debate, visited New York, Philadelphia, and other cities. Cultured easterners, like the cosmopolites of New Orleans, found his manners charming, his intellect sharp, his conversation interesting, and if his accents were unfamiliar, he found theirs equally strange. The great unwashed, of course, hailed him as one of their own heroes.

Back home the general tended his acres, supervised the breeding of his horses, built the new brick home for Rachel, supervised treaty-making with Indians whose lands still attracted westerners, watched over his district, and talked about retirement. Active duty, however, remained attractive because he might be needed for a campaign in the West, and the steady income helped him live in the style he enjoyed. In Washington, President Monroe faced problems that included a reduction in the armed forces resulting from cutbacks ordered by economy-minded congressmen. Monroe had one too many major generals and had to make a choice between Jackson and Jacob Brown. Both men had influential friends, but Jackson was a national hero whose explosive temper and contentious, if not formidable, personality were well known. Monroe talked with Eaton about appointing Jackson territorial governor of Florida; the idea appealed to Eaton because he and other friends of the general were speculating in land down there. Jackson was reluctant and Rachel was opposed, but, after assurances that he was not being eased out of his command, he accepted. After all he had been instrumental in acquiring the territory; he could help his speculating friends and use his patronage power in placing some of his unemployed junior officers.

The governor, armed with more power than any civil servant before or since, set out with his family and with the determination to stay only long enough to get the territorial government organized and working. The summer and early fall of 1821 were trying times. Spanish officials were expert procrastinators and profoundly resentful of Americans, especially Jackson whom they hated and feared. One contretemps led to another, and a final confrontation resulted in the impatient and angry Jackson jailing the Spanish governor, Don José Callava. When released Callava hastened to Washington to complain. The government Jackson established featured his major concept of democracy, which was that the state should provide even-handed justice for all—rich and poor, great and small. The governor left Pensacola on October 7, 1821; in eleven weeks he had organized a government and had it working.

The time and place when Jackson was exposed to the presidential itch went unnoticed and unrecorded, but some of his men, proud of serving with him in the War of 1812, extolled his qualities as a leader and mentioned him as a likely candidate from time to time. The general recalled years later that Edward Livingston mentioned it to him in 1816 or 1817. Less than a year after the war's end that shrewd pariah Aaron Burr picked him as a winner. After their return from Florida, Rachel complained that Senator Eaton and others talked too much about the presidency when they visited the Hermitage. The hero, for his part, showed a surprising modesty—even if feigned—when he snorted that he was not "damned fool enough" to think he could be elected.

A small circle of friends that came to be known as the Nashville Junto knew how to handle the general because they had known him for years. Included in this group were Overton, Eaton, William B. Lewis, Grundy, George W. Campbell, and Sam Houston. Eaton, from his base in Washington, wrote friends in the East and talked with others in Congress. Lewis and Overton had a local editor call attention to the old hero's availability, and Eaton arranged for reprints of the editorial to appear in western and eastern papers. Members of the junto wrote friends in neighboring states to complain about the evils of nominating candidates in congressional caucus. Lewis, in the spring of 1822, persuaded his father-in-law, Senator Montfort Stokes of North Carolina, and Colonel William Polk, wealthy land baron of North Carolina, to help in their state. When the Tennessee legislature met in the summer of 1822, the members endorsed Jackson and recommended him to the voters throughout the nation. The old hero calmly went about his business at the Hermitage and declared that he would not exert himself to win the presidency, but then he did not have to with the junto in operation. Of course his coyness was in keeping with the standards of the day.

Early in 1823, Eaton began writing his *Letters of Wyoming* wherein he presented Jackson as a nationalist and a man of the people who would carry on in the tradition of the Founding Fathers and "true republicanism of Revolutionary vintage." Jackson was free of a "consuming personal ambition" in contrast to the intriguing and manipulating quartet, Calhoun, Clay, Adams, and Crawford, each of whom panted for office. These "letters" received national circulation as one paper after another reprinted them. Jackson committees were organized around the country and encouraged mass meetings to endorse the old warrior. When notified that he was the choice of Pennsylvanians, Jackson, in his reply, indicated that he was a candidate.

The political cosmetologists had one last touch to make. In the fall of 1823, the Tennessee legislature had to elect a senator, and they had a choice between incumbent John Williams, a Crawford supporter, and

John Rhea. As the candidates jockeyed for position, Eaton and Lewis concluded that Rhea did not have a chance and only the general could defeat Williams. Jackson refused to lift a hand, but he did agree to serve if elected. This satisfied the plotters. Rhea withdrew and Jackson was elected. In Washington, Jackson lived with Eaton at O'Neale's place and joined the dinner circuit where he impressed the most fastidious with his dignity and urbanity. He dined with the Clays, Adamses, and Calhouns, and they dined with him. Jackson and Thomas Hart Benton, now a senator from Missouri, forgave each other and renewed their friendship. Senator Jackson attended to his routine business and was seldom absent from his seat. He must have been under considerable strain to keep his mouth shut because he joined in debate only four times. He did indicate that he favored a "judicious tariff" and that a national debt was not a blessing. All in all, the senator dispelled some of the doubts people held about his fitness for higher office.

Presidential politics, in 1824, was confused. Lines dividing the old Federalists and Jeffersonian Republicans had faded during the so-called era of good feeling; in fact the Federalists as a party went out of existence. Moreover, factionalism, regionalism, and personalities fragmented the Republicans. Monroe was in the position of having three aspirants for his office in his cabinet—Calhoun, Adams, and Crawford. The ever-ready Clay was speaker of the House. These men broke the precedents set by the first three presidents of appearing to let the office seek the man; they began their campaigns right after Monroe's re-election in 1820. Crawford had the support of the congressional caucus which in times past had selected candidates, so naturally his opponents attacked the system. Jackson, despite his comparatively late entry, had two strong points in his favor: he was a national hero and fitted into the mold of the "common man" whose success generally met the approval of the masses—of course Jackson had long been a member of the aristocracy that developed when Tennessee was the frontier. Calhoun, surveying the crowded field, decided to settle for the vice-presidency. In the election Jackson received a plurality of the popular vote but lacked a majority of the electoral votes. The members of the House of Representatives had to choose among the three top candidates. Clay was dropped because he ran fourth, and a serious illness all but eliminated Crawford. Jackson, Clay believed, was unfit for the office and would be a threat to his plans for 1828; he supported Adams as the lesser of two evils. The Tennessean gracefully accepted his defeat and ignored rumors of an agreement until Adams announced Clay's appointment as secretary of state. Jackson had little trouble, despite the absence of firm evidence, in believing the charge of "bargain and corruption," "sale and intrigue," or the union of "the Puritan and the Blackleg." Jackson had the satisfaction of casting one of the minority votes against the confirmation of Clay as secretary of state. The old hero resigned from the Senate in the fall of 1825, after Tennessee legislators nominated him again, because he did not want his enemies to charge that he used the position to promote his candidacy.

Jacksonians began looking toward 1828 immediately after Adams settled in the White House. From the Hermitage, Jackson maintained a voluminous correspondence filled with denunciations of the "corrupt bargain." Eaton, perhaps a model for later campaign managers, made many trips to raise money for financing newspapers; he helped Duff Green who made the *United States Telegraph* the leading Jackson paper. Overton and Lewis organized a committee of correspondence, also known as the Whitewashing Committee, that had counterparts in other cities. They supplied information to defend the old hero and attack his defamers. Political leaders realigned their forces. Martin Van Buren with his New York machine and Calhoun with his following went into the Jackson camp. In Congress, Benton and other friends did all they could to keep the coalition of Adams and Clay on the defensive.

As the election of 1828 approached, the Jacksonians had the advantage in organization and leaders. They also had the hero, but he was vulnerable. Instead of issues, personalities dominated the campaign which set an unequaled record for scurrility and defamation. Jackson was portrayed as an adulterer, murderer, and traitor based on Rachel's fouled-up divorce, his duels, the courts martial, and the Burr conspiracy; even the legitimacy of his birth was questioned. Adams, for his part, had to face the charges of "sale and intrigue" and having been a pimp for the czar when Adams was minister to Russia. Furthermore, westerners thought that he had been too willing to bargain away their rights at the Ghent negotiations in 1814 and that he was too kind to the Indians. Before the campaign ended, the old Republican party divided into Adams's National Republicans and Jackson's Democratic Republicans.

When the votes were counted, Jackson could take satisfaction that his support came from all sections of the nation, and the commonalty rejoiced that the man they considered one of their own had reached the pinnacle of success. At the Hermitage, Rachel worried while Eaton tried to prepare her for the role of First Lady. The venomous gossip, accusations, and lies circulated during the campaign were too much for her, and she died of a heart attack on December 22, 1828. The "gin'ral" was devastated but carry on he did. In the company of Lewis, Andrew Jackson Donelson, and others, he went by steamboat to Pittsburgh where he changed to stagecoach and proceeded to Washington. Thousands of friendly people turned out to greet the President-elect enroute, but his enemies were so vociferous and mortified by his victory that James K. Polk cautioned him not to expose himself to some vindictive and reckless opponent. One minister indicated his concern for Washington under Jackson when he chose his text, "'When Christ drew near the city he wept over it.'"

By the thousands hero-worshipers, job-hunters, and little people who wished him well gathered in Washington for the inauguration of the man they had elected President while members of the old order sneered and criticized the excessive display of democracy. Retiring President Adams, as his father had done in 1801, absented himself from the ceremonies. Jackson's inaugural address—Donelson, Lewis, and others helped write it—reflected his Jeffersonian beliefs; he wanted to liquidate the national debt; he paid his respects to states' rights; he reconciled the tariff with internal improvements; and he declared that the patronage system could be improved.

In putting together his cabinet Jackson tried to recognize the two factions that contributed to his success and thereby set the stage for trouble. He also insisted that he have one of his close friends in his official family; Hugh Lawson White of Knoxville turned him down, so he appointed Eaton secretary of war. Eaton had recently married—some people claimed on the President's order—Peggy O'Neale Timberlake, a vivacious widow whose social background did not qualify her for social intercourse with the ladies of the cabinet—so they thought. Emily Donelson, the President's niece and hostess and wife of "Jack" Donelson, his private secretary, agreed with the wives; she snubbed Peggy. Jackson had known Peggy since he boarded at her father's house; he equated her position with that of his beloved Rachel. The President ordered his cabinet members to get their wives under control, and he told Andrew (he never called him "Jack") and Emily that they had to accept Peggy. Secretary of State Van Buren, a widower, considered Eaton as an ally against Calhoun, and he won the friendship of the President by paying gallant attention to Peggy. The petticoat battle turned into a political war, so Jackson had to do something about his cabinet. He came to the conclusion that Calhoun was behind the plan to force Eaton out of the cabinet. Before "Eaton malaria" subsided, the Donelsons took a prolonged vacation in Tennessee, and Van Buren engineered changes in the cabinet by offering his resignation. Other members, including Calhoun's friends and Eaton, followed suit. Van Buren received an appointment as minister to Britain only to have Calhoun cast the deciding vote that prevented his confirmation. Jackson, who respected and liked the New Yorker, repaid him by choosing him as his running mate in 1832.

Jackson, as his predecessors and successors in office, did not rely wholly on his cabinet to advise him on administrative and political matters. He gathered an informal group of trusted and loyal friends who became known as the Kitchen Cabinet. The membership fluctuated, but the most influential were Amos Kendall, fourth auditor in the Treasury Department, later postmaster general; Lewis; Van Buren; Donelson; Roger B. Taney, attorney general, secretary of the treasury, and later chief justice; and Francis P. Blair, editor of the *Washington Globe*. The President listened to them and tempered their advice to accord with his convictions and mood. Van Buren became more influential as Jackson came to know him. When the President's health and the weather permitted, he enjoyed horseback rides accompanied by Van Buren, with whom he discussed the problems they faced. Jackson made important decisions only after careful study and consideration of alternatives. He asked for advice on important messages to Congress and vetoes, and he listened politely and attentively to men who differed with him and were frank. Once he decided on a course of action the debates ended.

The old hero entered the White House as a nominal Jeffersonian Republican, but with the passing of time and confronted with new problems, he added ideas and practices that came to be called Jacksonian Democracy. Indian removal, begun under Jefferson, accelerated, sometimes with the aid of a military escort. The President's attitude toward Indians was that of a land-hungry westerner; he seemed to have favored rights of states in handling the Indian problem, but he never had to face the issue directly. Economy in government and reduction of the national debt were almost a mania with him, and to his great satisfaction he discovered that he could pay off the debt in his second term. Internal improvements financed by the federal government he denounced as extravagant and claimed that they led to log-rolling schemes by congressmen; the fact that they were part of Clay's American System had something to do with his dislike. The President asked Van Buren to be on the lookout for an improvement measure that he could veto. The secretary spotted the Maysville Road bill which affected a twenty-mile stretch between Lexington and Maysville, Kentucky, and Jackson used his veto. The

President approved similar bills when he thought they had military value; this ambivalence led some wit to suggest that Jackson believed Clay would profit from the Maysville bill.

In 1829, the in-coming administration presented a condition some 11,000 government employees had not faced for three decades — a new party in power. Job security, tenure, and pensions were unknown in those days. Some of the bureaucrats were old and infirm, could not perform their duties, and should have been superannuated. Others thought they had property rights to their positions; some did not give an honest day's work for an honest day's pay; a minority drank on the job. These people naturally were frightened by Jackson's policy of "rotation in office," and National Republicans did all they could to exaggerate its evils. The President did believe that new people with fresh ideas and enthusiasm could improve the work of the departments and more than compensate for the loss of experienced employees; furthermore, after leaving office the people would take greater interest in government. In practice Jackson "rotated" about one-fifth of the employees, which compared favorably with Jefferson's record. Reform was needed in 1829, and Jackson made necessary changes. He undeservedly received credit as founder of the spoils system.

In foreign affairs Jackson scored a round of successes. The President got off to a good start when Van Buren suggested that he give a series of dinners for the diplomatic corps in Washington because he was not well known to the ministers and their governments. The old gentleman charmed his guests with his conversation, his manners, food, and wine; some of the credit should go to his French chef who was a holdover from Adams's administration. Jackson reached an agreement with the British to remove some mutual restrictions on trade so that ports in the West Indies could be opened to American ships. American interest in developing trade in the Far East was reflected in a treaty with Siam and the futile effort to make a treaty with Cochin China. With a little bullying Jackson persuaded Denmark and the Kingdom of the Two Sicilies to settle long standing spoliation claims. Since the days of Napoleon, the United States had similar grievances against France, and the President opened negotiations. When domestic politics resulted in the Chamber of Deputies not providing funds to pay the claims, Jackson spoke unkindly of France in his annual message; in fact, he rattled anchor chains in frigates. Members of the cabinet suggested that he tone down his message, and Jackson allegedly retorted, "No, gentlemen, I know them French. They won't pay unless they're made to." The French indicated their displeasure, and Jackson informed them that his message to Congress was none of their business. Britain offered to mediate, and in time Jackson apologized in a left-handed manner while France paid. Jackson, expansionist and nationalist that he was, kept Texas and California in mind, but he had no opportunity to fulfill his dream. In 1836, when the annexation of Texas may have been possible, he turned down the opportunity because he believed it was involved with the slavery question and therefore jeopardized the election of Van Buren.

The major issues Jackson confronted were nullification and recharter of the Bank of the United States; both resulted in his setting precedents for the use of executive powers that strong-willed and determined Presidents later found useful and to which they added when faced with crises. The controversy with South Carolinians had its origins in the Tariff of Abominations passed in 1828 to embarrass the Adams administration. High duties, southerners believed, increased the cost of the goods they bought on the protected market while they sold their commodities on the unprotected world market; Carolinians especially were incensed and used Calhoun's tract on states' rights to claim that a state could nullify acts of Congress. Jackson and Calhoun exchanged challenges at the Jefferson Day dinner in 1830; the President toasted the "Union" which he intended to preserve, while the vice-president drank to liberty which he considered above the Union. The showdown came in 1832 when the new tariff bill incorporated some objectionable features of the old. Hotheads in Charleston prepared to demonstrate how nullification could work. Calhoun, by this time, had been exposed as having been an enemy of Jackson back in 1818 when the Florida escapade came before the Monroe administration. Therefore Jackson reshuffled his cabinet to eliminate Calhoun's friends. The vice-president resigned to better serve his state in the Senate.

While "nullies" armed themselves, drilled, and orated, their more cool-headed neighbors conferred with friends in Washington. The President indicated that nullifiers could talk and demonstrate, but they could not shed blood. Jackson prepared to enforce the laws, as he was sworn to do, by ordering the navy to prepare for blocking Charleston harbor. Army officers at Forts Moultrie and Sumter suspected of being states' righters were replaced. Joel R. Poinsett, Jackson's man on the scene in South Carolina, received weapons that could be used, if needed, in street fighting. In the middle of December 1832, the President issued his proclamation on nullification after Livingston softened the tone of the original, but Jackson's meaning was clear: "Disunion by force is treason." Privately, the President assured Van Buren that he would "act with all forbearance," but he would not see law-abiding Carolinians mistreated; that would encourage disunionists everywhere. "Nullies" who shed blood would be tried for treason. "Nothing," the old man wrote, "must be permitted to weaken our government at home or abroad." To back up his stand, Jackson asked Congress to authorize his use of force — "the bloody bill" some people called it. State legislatures passed resolutions in support of the President, and nullifiers realized they stood alone. In early 1833 a compromise tariff bill proved to be acceptable, and resort to force was avoided. For the third time, a threat to dissolve the union was aborted.

The President's attitude toward banks was in some respects that of westerners. The Bank of the United States, he thought, was a monopoly that restricted credit for farmers, merchants, and other low income groups during hard times, but he might not have waged an all-out war had Nicholas Biddle, president of the bank, avoided involvement in presidential politics. The bank's charter did not expire until 1836, but in a conversation in November 1829 with Jackson about liquidating the national debt Biddle brought up the charter. Jackson made it plain that he doubted its constitutionality. While Jackson and some of his friends studied alternatives to the bank, Biddle helped congressmen and editors with loans, and even made John Overton a director in the Nashville branch; Daniel Webster and Clay had long been recipients of his largess. As the election of 1832 neared, Biddle decided to follow the advice of Clay, who needed an issue, and applied for a new charter that Congress granted. Jackson regarded the bill as a challenge. With the help of Donelson, Taney, Kendall, and Levi Woodbury, Jackson drafted a veto message in which he branded the bank as a "hydra of corruption" that bribed officials, that was partially owned by foreigners, that was not responsible to the people, and was unconstitutional. Clay and Biddle could not get the votes to override the veto. Jackson probably lost votes in the ensuing presidential election because of the bank, but he still was the old hero of the masses who re-elected him.

Faced with the impending demise of the bank, Jackson had to prepare a policy for handling federal deposits. He asked his cabinet and other advisers for ideas. Attorney General Taney immediately recommended that strong state banks be used because Biddle had not paid promptly in retiring the national debt. He had speculated in and profited from government bonds, bribed editors, and greatly increased loans, and the bank was unsafe. Kendall and Blair agreed. Secretary of the Treasury

Louis McLane took his time but finally announced that state banks were unsafe and a new bank should be created. He was transferred to the State Department, and William J. Duane replaced him in Treasury. Many state bankers, Kendall reported, feared Biddle, but he found enough strong banks willing to become depositories. Jackson, accordingly, explained his plan to his cabinet and found Lewis Cass, Duane, and McLane opposed. Jackson was not concerned with Duane's agreeing; he wanted him to enforce the order of withdrawal or resign. Soon thereafter the President fired Duane and appointed Taney, "who is . . . *with me in all points.*" Later Jackson declared, "I am ready with the screws to draw every tooth and then the stumpts." As Taney went about his business, Biddle created a financial crisis by sharply curtailing loans, and his friends in Congress tried to save the bank.

State banks—"Pet Banks" some people called them—expanded their issues of bank notes, and Biddle relaxed his restrictive policies so that loans became easily available. The people celebrated the return of "good times" that soon developed into a speculative orgy. With the federal debt paid, the government found itself with surplus funds, and Congress passed the distribution act to divide the money among the states; reluctantly Jackson signed it. This triggered a spending spree by the states and added to the problem. Public lands became prime speculative ventures that Senator Benton attempted to curb by requiring payment in gold or silver, but his bill failed to pass. The President, exercising his power, issued his famous executive order, the Specie Circular, which embodied Benton's idea. The circular reduced speculation, and with Jackson's other fiscal policies, so his critics claimed with 20-20 hindsight, contributed to the Panic of 1837.

Jackson did get out of Washington when his health and business permitted. In the summer of 1833, he followed precedent with a junket that took him into New England. He became the first President to ride in the new "Steam Carrs" when Baltimoreans met him twelve miles from the city. Easterners turned out to greet their hero. As Jackson's party neared Cambridge, President Josiah Quincy of Harvard College hastily convened the trustees to approve an honorary degree for him. John Quincy Adams, neither the first nor the last snobbish Harvardian, protested; but Quincy reminded him that people thought Jackson knew enough law to run the country, and Harvard could not say they were in error. Adams felt too disgraced to attend the ceremony where a semiliterate barbarian received such an honor. "Major Jack Downing" (Seba Smith), a newspaper humorist, reported that as Jackson finished his short acceptance speech he, "Downing," whispered, "give 'em a little Latin," and the newly-hooded Doctor Jackson added, "E pluribus unum, . . . my friends, sine qua non." On this same trip when Jackson and Van Buren reviewed troops in Boston, the latter's horse bolted only to stop "tail first against a fence." Jackson laughed as he commented that the vice-president was matched with a horse more non-committal than he. The President shortened his tour when he was stricken with one of his periodic hemorrhages. Later in the summer he relaxed under the off-shore breezes at the Rip Raps (Old Point Comfort, Virginia). His stay at the Hygeia Hotel from July 27 to August 22, 1833, cost $395.75. Included in his entourage were Andrew Junior and Sarah, Emily, Ralph E.W. Earle, three children, and five servants. His bar bill came to $118.50 for twelve bottles of champagne, brandy, gin, three gallons of whiskey, wines, and six bottles of olives at $1.50 each. He returned to the Hermitage in the summer of 1834 for a visit and left the White House in charge of William B. Lewis. In September he instructed Lewis "to say to the chamber maid to have all our beds clear of bedbuggs." Two years later on his way to inspect the restored Hermitage, he commented on the difficulty of travel. The roads were in wretched condition near "Salum," Virginia, where his carriage had broken axles; ten horses had pulled it from a mudhole; he covered ten miles in seven hours. Surely this experience should have made him more charitable toward internal improvements.

Jackson kept open house for his nieces, nephews, grand nieces and nephews, wards, all of their friends, his grandchildren, his friends, and their children. The White House rang with their merrymaking, and many "eagles" they cost him. Added to these were the guests who just happened to be calling at mealtime. On informal occasions family and guests gathered in the Red Room for preprandial drinks. The old patriarch joined them for a glass of wine and briefly exchanged pleasantries before dinner was served at four o-clock. A young marine lieutenant was invited to take pot luck one evening and had a choice of roast beef, cornbeef, boiled beef, or steak, followed by fish, more courses, then desserts; wines included sherry, maderia, and champagne. Formal dinners began at 7:30; the menu and wine list were longer. Probably be-

---

(*Above*): Sketch of the second inauguration of Jackson as President, 1833. From John Frost, *Pictorial Biography of Andrew Jackson*. (*Below*): An artist's rendition of Columbia, Tennessee, home town of James K. Polk. From A.W. Putnam, *History of Middle Tennessee*.

cause of his digestive ailments, the President had given up hard liquor years before he entered the White House and ate sparingly of rice, vegetables, and milk. For his family and guests, however, he bought wines, whiskey, and rum by the casks and barrels.

Jackson put in long hours going over papers and reports, conferring with his cabinet, dictating orders and letters, and seeing visitors who seem to have had easy access to his office. In many of his letters he referred to the lateness of the hour as he wrote. He prepared rough drafts of his messages, which Donelson and others smoothed out — and sometimes toned down as they did some of his letters. He listened attentively to his callers and usually saw their points before they explained them. "His reasoning," Amos Kendall said, "was like lightning." His ethics did not inhibit him from reading the secret journal of the Senate and writing a friend that Senator George Poindexter opposed an Indian treaty and "*this ought to be known in Mississippi, as his election comes on next fall.*" Sometimes the President seemed to pay too much attention to detail; when signing an appointment to the military academy, he expressed the wish that the boy would apply himself and do better than some of the Tennesseans recently in attendance. On another occasion he ordered Amos Kendall to investigate three employees of the Post Office Department who were accused of public drunkenness in a "cow-field," in the streets, and in a billiard parlor. If guilty, they were to be "promptly removed" for conduct unbecoming to gentlemen and officers of the government.

With the reorganization of his cabinet in 1831, Jackson eliminated the Calhoun faction and with the help of Van Buren, Blair, and others put together the party that soon came to be known as "Democratic." The old hero anointed "Little Van" as his heir apparent by choosing him as his running mate in 1832. The New Yorker was not popular in all parts of the country; in Tennessee, for example, John Bell and Hugh Lawson White joined the opposition. Calhoun and his states' righters were also active. Clay and the National Republicans denounced "King Andrew" and became the nucleus of the Whig party. In 1836, Democrats, meeting in Baltimore, ratified Jackson's choice, while Whigs relied on sectional candidates — White in the South, William Henry Harrison in the West, and Webster in the East — to throw the election into the House where one of them might win. The President and his men, nevertheless, triumphed with Van Buren's victory. Jackson not only left his party in control of the White House, but he left the Supreme Court in the hands of Chief Justice Taney and a Democratic majority that, while not reformist, at least modified some interpretations of John Marshall's court.

Three days after Van Buren's inaugural Jackson traveled homeward by train, coach, and steamboat. Cheering crowds met their hero along the way to wish him well. He arrived on March 25 with ninety dollars in his pocket (he had left in 1829 with $5,000) and a bad cough to find his hay lofts and corn cribs empty and his "blooded stock in bad order." When he regained his strength he intended to amuse himself "in riding over my farm and visiting my good neighbours, who, all but one, a new born Whigg, formerly my friend, has cheered and welcomed my return." To Jack Donelson he sent a "half Eagle" which was "half of my present means after paying for my corn . . . which ought to buy you three barrells of corn."

In retirement the old chieftain kept up a voluminous correspondence on national affairs with his friends in Washington. He became concerned about the safety of the "deposit Banks," the 30 percent interest farmers had to pay, and rampant speculating in land. When Blair lost a printing contract through the machinations of John Bell, Jackson twitted him for being "Bellised." Van Buren had Jackson's "Constitutional Carriage" (built from timbers from the famous frigate and a present from the people) shipped with a "quarter cask of old and excellent sherry." He asked to be remembered when it was consumed. Jackson graciously replied that he hoped the President and his friends could visit the Hermitage and join him in a "joyous glass of this much esteemed present." Jackson continued his running feud with John Quincy Adams, who set him off in 1838 when he brought to the attention of the House a letter in which Jackson had commented on troubles along the Mexican border; Jackson, demanding to know how Adams obtained the letter, claimed it had been stolen. Six years later, the old hero was "aroused" on receipt of a statement Adams made about the Texas boundary treaty of 1819; Adam's version was "*false, false, false, his diary to the contrary notwithstanding.*" Jackson dashed off his version and had it published in the *Nashville Union.* Later he thanked Blair for taking notice of "that lying old scamp, J.Q. Adams."

Jackson kept in touch with his up-and-coming friend, Congressman James K. Polk of Columbia, Tennessee, who had served as one of his leaders in the House. He invited Polk, in August 1837, to visit him for a day and a night to talk politics before setting out for Washington. The old hero encouraged him to run for governor two years later and was elated when Polk won. Jackson proved to be a poor vaticinator when he predicted that it would be a century before Tennesseans would allow themselves to be duped again by "such jesuitical hypocrites and apostates as Bell White and Co." Whigs were stronger in the state than Jackson would admit, and James C. "Lean Jimmy" Jones defeated Polk in his bid for a second term. Jackson showed his lack of respect when he referred to "Lean Jimmy" as "Mr. Jones, I cannot call him major for he never was a corporal." Anticipating the presidential campaign of 1840, Jackson called attention to his protégé's ambitions and mentioned him as a vice-presidential candidate who could get votes on the ticket with Van Buren. Since that failed to materialize, Jackson, as early as November 1843, again urged Van Buren to take Polk as his partner the next year because he "is the strongest, as well as the truest man that can be taken up in the south or west." When Polk received the nomination for President in 1844, Jackson quickly advised him to press the Texas question and to avoid a deal with Tyler Democrats because it would look like "bargain and intrigue."

After Polk's election, the old hero gloated that the "betting Whiggs" were broke; two neighbors had lost their horses and mules. Washington bound, Polk dutifully made a last pilgrimage to the Hermitage, where he and the master spent a day and two nights in "full and free conversation upon all matters and things." Respectfully but not at all reticent, Jackson asked favors for close friends. "Blairs Globe" should be retained as the administration's paper, and "William B. Lewis [used] to ferret out and make known to you all the plotts and intrigues Hatching against your administration." He thought that Donelson and Kendall could be appointed to diplomatic posts, and he asked for minor clerkships for several young relatives. Polk, he warned, should beware of Robert J. Walker. Patiently and skillfully Polk explained his points of view. He found positions for Donelson and the relatives; he appointed Walker secretary of the treasury. Polk firmly eliminated Blair so his friends could obtain control of the *Globe,* whose name was then changed to the *Washington Union.* Jackson accepted the President's explanations, but to Blair he declared that Polk had never shown more lack of "good common sense." Ironically, the last letter Jackson wrote was to Polk; he thanked him for getting a position for a relative; he was glad that the cabinet was united; and again he warned that Walker was dangerous.

Jackson continued to follow the fortunes of William B. Lewis who served him for so long. In the fall of 1839, their relations were somewhat strained when the general suggested that Lewis had become conservative and was an embarrassment to Van Buren. Furthermore, he still believed in the principle of rotation in office. Lewis should resign his position before he was fired. Lewis reminded Jackson of his services over the years; he wanted to stay in Washington until his young daughters finished their schooling. In their rather stiff exchanges each man assured the other of his everlasting friendship and loyalty. They eventually reconciled their differences, and Lewis helped arrange a loan from a Boston financier, which Jackson decided not to accept. During the campaign of 1844, Jackson denied the story circulated by "Whiggs" that "Col. Burr and the militant Federalists" has first proposed him for the presidency. Surely Lewis, one of the original members of the junto, smiled as he continued reading that the nomination "was the spontaneous movement of the demicracy." Later Jackson utilized Lewis's ferret-like ability to find a position in the bureaucracy for a young kinsman. The old man could not save his friend; in a last letter Jackson assured Lewis that Polk had not consulted him about firing the auditor and whoever said otherwise told a falsehood.

The correspondence in the post-presidential years between Jackson and Blair shows the mutual respect and feeling of friendship each had for the other. They were elated when Democrats triumphed over the "Whiggs," and their optimism overcame the disappointment that went with defeat as they waited for the next election. They were eloquent when they discussed the prospects of "Miss Emuckfa," a thoroughbred filly Jackson trained and sent to Blair. Jackson interceded with General Santa Anna to secure the release of a young man who had lived next door to Blair. During the campaign of 1844, Blair told Jackson that he had bet more than $22,000 on Polk because when Whigs bragged, he bragged back. Win or lose — he could afford to lose — he resolved never to bet again because "it is calculated to give one a bad character and ruin ones habits." "We rejoice," Jackson wrote after Polk's election, "that you in your coon hunt have secured as much *good fur* as will keep you and your family warm thro the winter." In 1842, when Jackson was under "pecuniary pressure," Blair came to his rescue with a loan of $10,000. Later Jackson wrote his will and stipulated how Blair should be repaid. The latter was "mortified" when he learned that Jackson had executed mortgage deeds for the loan; the general should not trouble himself about it.

Jackson's troubles stemmed from the bad judgment and bad management of Andrew Junior whose ventures never came up to expectations; the general with his high standards of family honor felt responsible for his son's debts. Jackson, like most farmers, was the eternal optimist about next year's crops, but late frosts in the spring, droughts or floods in the summer, and early freezes in the fall coupled with fluctuating prices resulted in his income usually being less than he anticipated.

Then, too, cotton fields at the Hermitage seem to have suffered from over-cropping. In the fall of 1844 when the general was embarrassed by his inability to pay interest on Blair's loan, his friend assured him that he could pay at his convenience and not to worry. Three months before he died, Jackson wrote that he and Sarah wept when they received Blair's offer to lend enough money to consolidate his debts — really Andrew Junior's. He needed $7,000, and he would give a "morgage" on 1,700 acres adjoining the Halcyon plantation on which the editor already held a "morgage." Soon thereafter John C. Reeves wrote that he had talked with Blair and Jackson could have five times the amount he requested. "Mr. Blair and myself are indebted to you *for all we are worth.*" Apparently the general did not live long enough to take advantage of Blair and Reeves's offer to consolidate his debts which included a loan of $7,000 advanced in 1841 by his old friend in New Orleans, J.B. Plauché.

Despite his chronic poor-mouthing, Jackson died solvent — at least according to historian Stanley F. Horn. Jackson owed Blair $15,000 and "an unnamed sum to General [Plauché]." He owned the Hermitage which had some 1,200 acres and "about 100 negroes besides stock of all kinds." Junior sold the plantation in Mississippi for $40,000, from which he paid off $21,000 in debts and had $19,000 in cash. Jackson's estate, clear of debt, amounted to $150,000 — he always insisted that basically he was solvent.

Jackson did not have good health after 1813. He had not recovered from wounds received in the gun fight with Jesse Benton when he began the campaign against the Red Sticks and developed dysentery that was to plague him for the remainder of his life. In his letters he frequently referred to his headaches, pains, chills, and fever. For relief he resorted to calomel, bleeding, and sugar of lead — an astringent he used internally and externally. He may have suffered from mercury and lead poisoning. He liked to prescribe home remedies and patent medicines for his friends. His favorite "Matchless Senative" relieved "pulmonary symptoms," headache, and earache and helped the patient cough up "fleme." With a glass of wine or toddy it would calm the mind and keep it "free from perplexing thoughts" — all for $2.50 per bottle.

When Jackson began building the new Hermitage for Rachel in 1819, he did not think that he would live long enough to enjoy it, but he was a stubborn man who kept going on sheer will power. He may have developed tuberculosis of the lungs and probably of the bone. During his presidency he suffered from many hemorrhages, and in the last months he did not leave his bedroom. In retirement his physical condition steadily deteriorated, but his mind remained active. With his other infirmities and a worn-out body, dropsy developed and the old hero died on June 8, 1845.

Had Old Hickory lived but four more years he would have been proud of his protégé who successfully completed some of the work begun in the days of Jackson — especially the extension of the national boundary to the Pacific Ocean.

3. Tennessee's Second President, Punctilious James

James Knox Polk, the eleventh President of the United States, may best be classified under the heading *sui generis* because he was indeed in a class to himself, unique, and peculiar. Aloof and reticent, with few close friends, he deliberately became a professional politician, rose through the ranks, and entered the White House after two major setbacks that would have discouraged less ambitious men. Elected President in 1844, he began his administration with the intention of serving one term and with four goals in mind. He wanted to settle the Oregon boundary dispute, acquire California, lower the tariff, and re-establish the independent treasury system. He is unique in that he did what he set out to do and went home.

Polk (1795–1849), born in Mecklenburg County, North Carolina, was a member of the large and prolific Polk clan that included wealthy and influential cousin William who owned thousands of acres in what was soon to become the State of Tennessee. Grandfather Ezekiel, surveyor and well-to-do farmer, had itching feet and suffered from the pangs of land hunger. Father Sam was an industrious and ambitious yeoman on the make. Ezekiel and several members of his family moved into Tennessee in 1803. Two or three years after the Cherokees surrendered land on the Duck River (the same land Jackson had advised Robert Hays to get all he could in 1798), the Polks moved to Maury County where Sam and his family joined them in the latter part of 1806. Ezekiel and Sam prospered and acquired extensive holdings in West Tennessee, while in Maury County the Polk acorns adorned many a gate post.

In the meantime, Jim started to school, heard politics discussed in the family circle, worked on the farm, cleared new ground, and sometimes accompanied his father when he surveyed lands "in the Western District." When he was sixteen, Jim, accompanied by his father, rode 230 miles to Danville, Kentucky, where Dr. Ephraim McDowell, famed frontier surgeon, removed gallstones without benefit of anesthesia; the experience made him healthier and may have contributed to the development of his character—at least it did not traumatize him.

Jim found outdoor work not to his liking and clerking in a store to be irksome, so he asked his father for an education. He attended an academy in Murfreesboro for two years, overcame his academic deficiencies, and in the fall of 1815 crossed the mountains to attend the University of North Carolina. Young Polk did so well on his entrance examinations that the faculty permitted him to enroll as a second-semester sophomore.

As an undergraduate, Polk became a member of a literary society whose minutebooks show that he could be one of the boys, and he held several offices while he sharpened his skills as a debater who effectively used logic and facts. The records do not show that his extramural activities involved wine, women, and song; presumably a young man of twenty—even Jim Polk—would not neglect this aspect of an education. His socializing with classmates and visiting the homes of cousin William and other relatives improved his manners to the point that he was "punctilious." Jim Polk avoided involvement in the student bomb-plot of 1816. The self-discipline and studious habits he developed early in his quest for an education resulted in his graduating with first honors in 1818.

Soon after he returned to Tennessee, Polk went to Nashville, where he read law under the watchful eyes of Felix Grundy, former congressman, a member of the state legislature, and an able politician with one of the largest practices in criminal law in the state. With his mentor's help Jim became a senate clerk on September 20, 1819. For six dollars a day—a legislator earned four—he kept track of bills, reports, resolutions, and other papers; he began learning the legislative facts of life and laid a firm foundation for a political career.

Polk passed his bar examination in the spring of 1820 and opened his law office in Columbia. At this time, according to historian Charles Grier Sellers, Jim informed his relatives that they could now call him "James." This manifestation of his concept of personal dignity was in keeping with the mature personality he developed in the next few years, a personality that featured self-discipline and extreme formality. These traits could handicap a young attorney with political ambitions, but Polk learned to appear affable, cordial, and a good fellow as he rode the circuit that included the county seats of Pulaski, Lawrenceburg, Shelbyville, and Fayetteville. He also joined a local militia company. Picayune legal fees he augmented by doing title work for his father and cousin William. Sam also made James a partner in some of his land deals in West Tennessee.

In 1822, Polk, who had been brought up on the principles of Jefferson, launched his political career by becoming a candidate for the state legislature. He resorted to a man-to-man canvass and had to ride over the county soliciting support of individual farmers and squires. Perhaps the muscles of his saddle-hardened fundament never relaxed until he seated himself in the "President's House" twenty-three years later. In keeping with the spirit of the times Polk catered to the palates of the "sovereigns" when he treated his followers in one district to twenty-three gallons of brandy, whiskey, and cider. Elected to the lower house, Polk steered clear of irrevocable commitments to the factions squabbling over banks and land speculation. Not until legislators came to the election of a United States senator in the fall of 1823 did Polk fully commit himself. The President-makers, John H. Eaton and William B. Lewis, in a desperate maneuver to defeat Senator John Williams persuaded General Jackson to let his name be used. Polk voted for the old hero and became a full-fledged Jacksonian. This was not difficult for the young and ambitious politician. Jackson, a long-time friend of Sam Polk, had watched James mature. Both were Jeffersonians who opposed nominations by congressional caucuses, banks, and certain classes of land speculators. Old Hickory was a self-made frontier aristocrat; young Polk was in the process of becoming a professional politician and a member of the landed gentry with the help of his father.

According to an undocumented story (which conforms to Jackson's reputation as a matchmaker), Polk asked one day in 1823 how he could succeed in politics. The first thing, said the general, was to stop his philandering and get married. Polk asked which of his friends he should choose. Jackson recommended the one who would not give trouble and who was qualified by education, wealth, family, and health; he added that Polk knew her well. Polk identified her as Sarah Childress and declared that he would ask her at once.

Sarah Childress (1803–1891) was the daughter of Joel Childress, a prominent and well-to-do farmer and businessman of Murfreesboro. Her father believed in educating his daughters and sent them to school in Nashville and to the Moravian academy in Salem, North Carolina. Sarah and James became acquainted when he studied in Murfreesboro, and they began courting when he returned as senate clerk. Their wed-

---

Early paintings of James K. Polk and his wife, Sarah Childress Polk, done in the 1830s. Courtesy of the Polk Memorial Association.

ding on January 1, 1824, was one of the great social successes of the year in Middle Tennessee.

Sarah's contemporaries described her as intelligent, lively, gracious, kindly, dignified, and a good politician and businesswoman. When her husband went to Washington, she usually accompanied him. Sarah became a favorite in Washington society, where she matched wits with the leading politicians, one of whom described her husband as the second most henpecked congressman in the city. Her dinner parties promoted her husband's career. She had a sense of humor so she could tease James during the bank fight in 1834 when he weighted down their luggage with specie to pay their travel expenses. The "genteel wetting" she received when she had to be rescued from a stagecoach stranded in a flooded stream was the greatest adventure of her life. When James took to the hustings in the long hot summers of 1841 and 1843, Sarah stayed home, read the mail, framed replies, and kept him informed of the activities of friends and foes. All of this helped prepare Sarah for her future role as First Lady.

Polk's success as a state legislator whetted his appetite for higher office; in 1825, he became a candidate for Congress. With the support of Jackson's friends, Polk defeated Andrew Erwin, one of the general's influential enemies. During the next fourteen years he rose to national prominence by doing his homework in Washington and by developing superb political skills which included deviousness, manipulating people, being non-commital at proper times, and learning patience. He stayed in office because he served his constituents well. Polk kept the farmers abreast of events by sending copies of documents and speeches by the hundreds. Requests for appointments to West Point, jobs for surveyors, and changes for mail and stage routes he handled with dispatch. He was a "friend of the veterans" who applied for pensions. Polk had a network of correspondents who kept him informed of the day-by-day alignments of friends and enemies at the crossroad stores in his district.

During his first term, Congressman Polk was more concerned with promoting Jackson than in legislating. In the latter activity, however, he followed the principles of proper Jeffersonians. He ate regularly with John C. Calhoun, Hugh Lawson White, and others whose goals, principles, and ambitions were to clash with his in the years ahead. In the late 1820s they worked for Jackson, and the older men spotted Polk as a man with a bright future. Polk kept the general well informed on affairs in Washington; their relations were such that toward the end of the campaign in 1828 Polk could advise the wrathful Jackson not to take direct action against his caluminators. After the election, Polk helped arrange Jackson's journey to Washington and worked on plans for the inauguration.

Polk continued his political education during Jackson's first term. He avoided Eaton malaria by leaving the outspoken Sarah in Columbia, and he foiled an investigation by William B. Lewis, Jackson's ferret, who suspected Tennessee congressmen of being unfriendly toward Van Buren. Polk led the opposition against the Maysville Road bill and defended Jackson's veto.

As tension mounted over the tariff, Polk shifted from the Foreign Affairs Committee to Ways and Means where his parliamentary skills, capacity for details, analytical powers, and pro-Jackson stance could be better used. When South Carolinians tentatively tested nullification, Polk suppressed his states' rights beliefs and supported his chief. Thus he became a leading Jacksonian, but not all of Polk's colleagues considered him a strong party leader at this time. Sam Houston wryly observed in the waning minutes of the session on March 3, 1833, when floor managers could not stem the flow of verbiage, that Polk's weakness resulted from his "use of water as a beverage."

Polk went home in the spring of 1833 to campaign for re-election. He found that his opposition to the Bank of the United States had made him a prime target of the friends of the "monster of corruption" who flooded his district with pro-bank and anti-Polk propaganda. Polk successfully explained his votes on the bank and other issues and with information Andrew Jackson Donelson unlawfully obtained from confidential documents proved his opponent to be anti-Jackson. His constituents elected him for the fifth time.

While campaigning for re-election Polk had advancement on his mind. In an unusually frank letter he reminded William B. Lewis of Speaker Andrew Stevenson's being slated for a diplomatic post. Friends suggested that Polk should be the next speaker. Tennessee, Lewis apparently indicated, was overly represented in national affairs. The speaker, Polk fired back, should be *"true"* and one *"never suspected"* of being anything but a Jacksonian, and, furthermore, friends of the administration had voluntarily suggested that he seek the post. Cave Johnson and Felix Grundy recommended him to their friends in other parts of the country. Jackson intimated to James Walker, Polk's brother-in-law, that he too wanted Polk in the speaker's chair. As events developed, Jackson delayed Stevenson's appointment, so Polk returned to Washington to become chairman of the Ways and Means Committee.

Polk immediately took the lead in the continuing battle with friends of the bank. Well-armed with damaging documents and statistics from the bank's records, some secretly furnished by Jackson, Polk spoke against recharter and justified the use of state banks. Widely circulated, the speech became source material for Democratic editors and orators, although crotchety John Quincy Adams said that Polk had only "confidence, fluency, and labor" to qualify as an orator.

In the spring of 1834, Polk had the votes to carry his point and was generally acknowledged as the administration leader in the House. Stevenson resigned at the end of the session, and the selection of his successor revealed the wide division among Democrats. In the contest between John Bell and Polk, Whigs, Democrats who favored the bank, and Calhoun's states' righters united to elect Bell.

Jackson's choice of Martin Van Buren as his successor troubled many Democrats and especially Tennesseans, many of whom favored Hugh Lawson White. When Polk campaigned for his sixth term in 1835, he satisfied his homefolks without alienating Jackson. Polk did not mention Van Buren and referred to White as a friend he could support if he won the nomination. The people in Middle Tennessee, he insisted, did not send him to Congress to help choose a President; they made their decisions at the ballot box. If the election went to the House, he would vote as the people in the district voted. Polk won, but "White, Bell, & Co." put Newton Cannon in the governor's chair and dominated the legislature. While Polk continued his quest for the speakership, Jackson and Donelson kept the luke-warm Blair and his *Globe* in line. With the help of the Van Burenites, the Tennessee congressman defeated his bitter enemy and achieved his immediate goal in December 1835.

Polk took up his gavel at a time when changes were under way. Already regarded as the spokesman for Old Hickory, he was accepted as the party leader in the House, the first of his kind, whose responsibility involved promoting and defending the administration's program. The Democratic party was divided among the Jackson-Van Buren faction, extreme states' righters, and the anti-Jackson group headed by White and Bell who leaned toward Whiggery. Among the voices of reformers could be heard the ever-louder tones of abolitionists whose petitions old man Adams gleefully and dutifully introduced. Whigs naturally gave trouble, while Bell, Balie Peyton, and Henry Wise were personal enemies who tried to provoke a duel with Polk. The speaker had mastered the rules and procedures; he recognized the nuances of the House; he was both tactician and strategist. He controlled his temper and ruled with firmness. Polk had little trouble with administration bills; he packed the committees, and he had the votes.

The presidential election of 1836 divided Democrats in Tennessee. Jackson's enemies, led by White and Bell, persuaded many Democrats that Van Buren did not deserve their support. The Whigs' strategy was to use three regional candidates that they hoped could win enough votes to throw the selection of the President into the House of Representatives. Judge White, one of the candidates, embarrassed and dismayed Jackson and his followers by carrying the state. Polk returned to Washington, where he helped close the Jackson administration. Demands for investigation of Jackson's alleged wrong-doings he turned over to committees packed with friends who promptly cleared the President. Donelson could not be in Washington for Van Buren's inauguration, so he asked the Polks to look after the ailing Jackson on his homeward journey.

Events of the late 1830s forced Polk to make hard decisions that affected his career. Although he had little trouble getting re-elected in 1837, other Democrats were not so fortunate and Whigs controlled the state. Because of Polk's strength in his district, his prominence in Washington, and his friendship with Jackson, he began to be recognized as the Democratic leader in Tennessee.

Polk found himself at the fork in the road that led to the White House. The direct route via the vice-presidency was a bit crowded; he decided that a little detour on the gubernatorial route would bring him back to the main road ahead of his competitors. He probably could have returned to Congress where Whigs in all likelihood would be in the ascendancy and deflate his ego by unseating him as speaker. Rumors circulated back home that he had his eyes on the vice-presidency, and Democrats mentioned him as a logical candidate for governor. Polk was noncommittal, but some editors began calling attention to his availability as a running mate with Van Buren. Polk went home in the summer of 1838, conferred with friends, and at a big rally in Murfreesboro announced that he yielded to the importunities of the rank and file of the Democratic party. He would be a candidate for governor in 1839. He wanted strong Democrats running for the legislature and Congress, and he asked Jackson to encourage and support them. As a warm-up for the campaign, Polk took advantage of the fall visit to his plantation to attend rallies in ten counties in West Tennessee, where he found "a great revolution in public sentiment." He returned to Washington for his last session in the House by way of East Tennessee to make speeches in a number of towns.

Polk hit the campaign trail in April 1839 and spoke in almost all, if not all, the county seats and at many country stores before the August election. A polished speaker with a facile mind, Polk scored on the pedestrian Cannon as he emphasized national issues and touched briefly on state issues as he hedged on internal improvements and the state-owned bank. Polk and his fellow Democratic candidates aroused their followers and attracted others who had strayed, so they turned out in larger numbers than in recent years. Polk won with some 2,500 votes to spare, six Democrats were elected to Congress, and the party controlled the legislature. Hailed as the redeemer, if not the messiah, of Tennessee Democrats, Polk became more attractive as a vice-presidential candidate in 1840.

Governor Polk found his duties to be ceremonial and clerical because the state constitution severely limited executive powers. At least the work helped satisfy his passion for minutiae. He tried, with some success, to work as party leader and to guide the legislature as he had the House. Polk attempted to get the factions to work together, and he apparently masterminded Grundy's return to the Senate and the replacement of Senator White with Alexander Anderson. The governor had trouble with head-strong legislators on running the state-owned bank — no one thought it socialistic in those days — bond issues, and internal improvements.

Polk had ample time to think of the vice-presidency while friends worked to get his name recognized throughout the land. State senator Samuel Hervey Laughlin introduced resolutions of endorsement. Jeremiah George Harris, editor of the *Nashville Union* (the major Jackson paper in the state), sharpened his quill. George Bancroft dropped hints to editors in New England. General Jackson assured Francis P. Blair that Polk could carry Tennessee for the ticket and he would serve only four years because the office "cannot have any charms for him." Cave Johnson and Tennesseans in Washington also worked for the governor. Because many men wanted the office, the national Democratic convention made no nominations in 1840 and left the choice to the voters in the states to throw the election into the Senate. Eventually all of the would-be candidates withdrew and left Vice-President Richard M. Johnson without opposition. Voters, as they usually do during hard times, blamed the party in power and elected Whig William Henry Harrison, who also carried Tennessee.

Frightened by the Whig triumph, Polk prepared for his campaign of '41 with words of encouragement for Democrats and urged tighter organization of party lines down to the civil districts. Whigs turned to James Chamberlain Jones, a well-to-do farmer and legislator who had attracted attention at political rallies. He weighed 125 pounds, stood six feet, two inches tall, and was called "Lean Jimmy." In the joint canvass that turned out to be the greatest road show in Tennessee, oratorical efforts of the candidates consumed more than two hours each and then rejoinders and replies took more time. Polk tried to feature national issues and the principles on which he stood as governor. Jones was witty, droll, folksy, and never let the truth interfere with the charges he made about Polk in particular and Democrats in general. Polk, dignified, experienced, and able, could not cope with the uninhibited Jones. According to one Democrat, "Polk tried to talk some sense to damn fools and made an ass of himself." He lost by about 2,600 votes, although he reduced the Whig vote of 1840.

Polk, the professional politician unemployed for the first time in his life, retreated to Columbia to regroup his forces. He kept up his correspondence with friends throughout the nation and resumed the practice of law. He entertained Van Buren when he came through on a fence-mending tour of southern states. Still the leader in Tennessee, Polk looked forward to the next election to prove his strength. The second canvass of Polk and Jones entertained as many Tennesseans as the first and yielded the same results. Polk lost by approximately 3,800 votes. The parties were almost evenly divided in the state.

Polk's financial affairs were in as great a disarray as his political career. Elected to Congress in 1825, Polk soon learned that his per diem of eight dollars plus travel and fees from his curtailed legal practice did not permit him to live in the style he enjoyed, and he turned to farming to supplement his income. After his father's death Polk began clearing a 970-acre tract in Fayette County—in the "Western District"—with an overseer and fifteen slaves, some of whom he inherited. His was a modest operation—and so were his returns. He sold out in 1834 for $6,000 and with his brother-in-law, Dr. Silas M. Caldwell, as a partner bought 880 acres in Yalobusha County, Mississippi, for $8,800. At the time he owned seventeen slaves worth $16,000. Polk soon acquired full ownership of the property and added to it. He was an absentee owner, never a satisfactory role, and his overseers ran the place. Twice a year, in the spring and fall, James and Sarah inspected the plantation and visited relatives enroute. For twenty-five years income fluctuated from $3,500 to $6,300 per year.

Demands on politicians were many, and Polk as leader of Democrats in Tennessee and as governor all but overextended his credit by subsidizing party papers and incurring other obligations. His living expenses in Nashville exceeded his annual salary of $2,000. He left office in 1841 owing over $10,000, with James Walker, a sharp businessman, exhorting him to get his finances in order and to quiet his creditors by paying them off at the rate of $2,000 a year. This he did with profits from his plantation and by resuming the practice of law. He wanted to sell the plantation, but Sarah convinced him that they would need it in their old age. In 1842, Polk went to Washington to check on politics and to Philadelphia and New York with the idea of selling some of his undeveloped land in West Tennessee or to use it as collateral for a loan. Eastern bankers, however, were not interested.

At his nadir, Polk the redeemer appeared to be the unredeemable. Twice defeated in his home state, he could have trouble convincing fellow Democrats that he added strength to the ticket as a vice-presidential candidate, but his ambition and drive were undiminished. Polk met with friends in Nashville on the night of October 2, 1843, to discuss his strength and weakness. Soon thereafter Democrats in a state convention endorsed him. Cave Johnson in Washington pressured Van Burenites. The ailing Jackson did his bit while Polk kept busy with his correspondence.

Before Polk retired from Congress, the annexation of Texas coupled with slavery had become an issue that Jackson had side-stepped. In 1844, expansionists spoke in terms of Texas and Oregon while their thoughts roamed farther afield. Some spoke in terms of "manifest destiny." Abolitionists and less radical anti-slavery groups had increased their numbers and raised their voices while southerners, equally loud, defended their economic institutions. Clay, with the Whigs in line, failed to detect a strong Texas breeze and decided against annexation on the ground that it would lead to war with Mexico. Van Buren, front runner among the Democrats, also announced his opposition to annexation. Polk, more in tune with western and southern Democrats and proper Jacksonian that he was, announced, when queried by a committee, that he favored the "re-annexation" of Texas.

Democratic delegates assembled in Baltimore faced hard decisions. Lewis Cass of Michigan had strong support in the West. After Van Buren misread the auguries, Levi Woodbury of New Hampshire and James Buchanan of Pennsylvania broke out with a presidential rash, and their supporters were active. So it was that Polk's staunch friends among the Tennesseans—Gideon J. Pillow, Sam Laughlin, Andrew Jackson Donelson, William G. Childress, and Cave Johnson—had a number of people with whom to bargain for their man, who sought only the second place on the ticket; the other eight delegates, including Andrew Johnson, were not dependable. Van Buren's stand on Texas prevented his getting the necessary two-thirds majority vote, and the convention deadlocked. Polk's men took advantage of their opportunities, persuaded the warring factions to compromise in favor of the Tennessean, who became the first "dark horse" President (in that he was not openly a candidate for the top office when the convention met) and the first to have news of his nomination sent by telegraph — from Baltimore to Washington. For the platform, Democrats reaffirmed the principles of Jefferson and Jackson and, ignoring the weakness of claims to previous ownership, called for the re-annexation of Texas and re-occupation of Oregon.

The campaign of '44 provided some excitement. Whigs tried to belittle Polk by asking, "Who is James K. Polk?" when they were well aware of his congressional record. Amos Kendall, a keen Jacksonian, may have shared Whiggish denigrations when he observed, "It is fortunate that after the surrender of Mr. Van Buren, the convention concentrated on one so unexceptional as Mr. Polk." Some enthusiastic Democratic editors and lusty partisans wanted all of Oregon to 54°40'. Polk, in an attempt to harmonize the factions in his party, announced that he would serve only one term. Following long-established precedent for presidential candidates, Polk stayed close to home and succeeded — as he could be expected to do — in keeping his plans to himself and thereby alienated no one while his friends in the various sections of the nation assured the voters that he was right and safe on issues they deemed important. Clay had trouble with the expansionists and the anti-slavery groups. The latter launched the Liberty party with James G. Birney as their candidate. Polk, who had won one close election and lost two by comparatively small margins, evened his score by winning the most important with 38,367 popular votes to spare; the electoral vote was 170 to 105. The Liberty party helped by taking anti-slavery Whigs away from Clay, especially in New York state.

The President-elect's first concern was his cabinet. To avoid the troubles of Monroe and Jackson, whose advisers with presidential ambitions embarrassed the Presidents, Polk, in letters of invitation to prospective cabinet members, clearly stated that he expected them to be cordially cooperative, to attend closely to their work, and to resign if they became candidates for higher office. For his part, Polk declared, he would not take sides or use patronage to promote the candidacy of any Democrat

who sought the nomination in 1848. He conferred with Jackson and others on appointments, and in the process he tried to reconcile factional differences. He chose his close friend Cave Johnson for postmaster general, and John Y. Mason, college classmate, served as attorney general and subsequently headed the Navy Department.

The President maintained friendly relations with his cabinet while he put them to work and looked over their shoulders. He met with them twice a week and always was available for private consultations. He conferred with them on all important questions, called for their opinions, listened to their advice, and made his decisions which they accepted, perhaps with mental reservations. Individually and collectively they helped with his messages and used their influence with members of Congress in getting votes for the administration's bills. Secretary of State James Buchanan sometimes acted up, but Polk handled him with patience and made the most of his talents; once the President had to warn his secretary of state to attend to his duties or he would find a "lion in his path." Toward the end of his term Polk complained that Buchanan's maneuverings toward the presidency were an embarrassment and that his advice was no longer reliable. A few months before leaving office Polk smugly remarked in his diary that he had conducted the government without the aid of Secretary of the Treasury Robert J. Walker and Secretary of War William L. Marcy because of their long absences from Washington. He had mastered the duties of subordinate officers and had "probably given more attention to details than any of my predecessors." Only occasionally did he need information or advice from his cabinet.

Polk began his administration prejudiced against the bureaucracy. Secret reports from trusted clerks about the "indifferent" attitude of many bureaucrats confirmed his belief that the government employees did little work. The worst cases, Polk believed, were no-good Whigs and Federalists. Polk became "vexed" and "spoke sharply" to the adjutant general when he learned that vacancies for commissioned officers were held open for the graduating class of the military academy; the President filled the vacancies by giving field commissions to privates who had distinguished themselves. On another occasion Polk chided the Treasury Department for taking two days to supply information that should have been provided within an hour.

A Currier print of Polk done during the presidential campaign of 1844. Courtesy of Special Collections, University of Tennessee Library.

Polk did not ask more of clerks and departmental heads than he demanded of himself, but he seemed to take masochistic satisfaction in working long hours. He rose early, took a morning walk, opened his office to any and all callers, dined about four in the afternoon, took another stroll, and then returned to his cluttered "table" which he seldom cleared before retiring. The President complained that the presidency is "no bed of roses," but he had himself primarily to blame. As a conscientious workaholic, he used a snowy Christmas day to dispatch "a mass of business which had accumulated" on his table. Polk's conception of his role as President caused him to receive hordes of office seekers, beggars, promoters of charities, and assorted nuts. Generally he was gentle, courteous, and firm in explaining that he had neither jobs nor alms to give. Privately, he sarcastically referred to able and patriotic men who wanted to serve their country by holding government sinecures. After one difficult day, the President "jestingly" remarked to his private secretary—his only helper and whose salary he paid—that he needed "one of Colt's revolving pistols to clear" the office so he could "attend to . . . public duties."

In dealing with patronage matters Polk was no more ruthless than his contemporaries; however, he had definite ideas on the subject. He also had several personal grudges to settle. An apt but undocumented story still circulates in Lawrence County about the two rural postmasters who opposed him in 1844; he promised to fire them, and after his inauguration they were among the first to go. Despite the recommendations of Jackson, Polk terminated William B. Lewis and forced Francis P. Blair to sell the *Globe* to Thomas Ritchie and others who changed the name to the *Washington Union*. Blair had not helped him get the vice-presidential nomination in 1840; he had not publicized Polk's endorsement by the state legislature. Blair considered Polk finished after his gubernatorial defeat and had not helped him in 1844. Polk had firm ideas about qualifications for federal judges; they had to be "original Democrats and strict constructionists." No Johnny-come-lately would do because he had "never known . . . a Federalist who had after arriving at the age of 30 professed to change his opinions." The President "suppressed" his indignation when two congressmen wasted his and their time wrangling about a commission for a second lieutenant in the regular army; he re-

A scene of the crowd at Polk's inauguration on a rainy day in March 1845. Courtesy Library of Congress.

minded them that they were sent to Congress to legislate and not to "dictate" to him.

Polk, who had long suffered with severe anal pains caused by Buchanan, became angry when the secretary selected an anti-administration paper in Rochester to publish government notices. Dissatisfied with Buchanan's letter revoking the arrangement, Polk provided the secretary with two drafts and told him to take his choice. The angry and frustrated executive toward the end of his term vowed, if God gave him the health and time in retirement, to write "the secret and hitherto unknown history of the workings of the Government" in respect to the time-wasting patronage problems.

Polk took office with two major domestic reforms on his agenda. He wanted a lower tariff and an independent treasury—"constitutional treasury" he called it. Democrats controlled both House and Senate, but they were divided on such issues as internal improvements, tariff, and slavery. Polk developed as a leader concomitantly with the evolution of a strong two-party system, and he came into power with definite ideas about running the government. As President he represented all of the people in contrast to the relatively small constituencies of representatives and senators, and he was responsible for guiding his party in legislative matters. He knew how to use presidential messages to appeal over the heads of congressmen to mold public opinion. He even took time to write articles for the *Union*. In "full conversations" with friendly and unfriendly congressmen, he used cajolery, threats, patronage, and compromises—everything but charm which he did not possess—to round up votes. Polk had little trouble getting the independent treasury re-established, but it may have indicated, as his major biographer suggested, that the people faced a new era and new issues.

Downward revision of the tariff was more difficult because Democrats in New York and Pennsylvania wanted to protect their growing industries and people in the old Northwest wanted internal improvements financed by import duties. Secretary Walker drafted the bill designed to fulfill Democratic promises, and it was introduced early in 1846. While the measure was in the legislative mill, manufacturers held a great fair in Washington to display their wares. Polk, unimpressed after a tour of the grounds, claimed that the exhibitors tried to intimidate congressmen and to propagandize against the low tariff. The President marshalled his forces and enjoyed his victory when the "great measure of reform" passed in mid-summer.

Americans did not want all of the land in the world or even an empire beyond the seas, but they did want the land adjacent to theirs. A growing population and an agricultural economy required more land. The purchase of Louisiana resulted in extensions of the boundaries to the Rocky Mountains and beyond and soon thereafter venturesome Americans met Britishers in the Oregon country. Unable to agree on a boundary — Americans wanted the line of the 49th parallel to the Pacific to get a good harbor in Puget Sound — Britain and the United States in 1818 compromised for joint occupation and nine years later extended the agreement. While maritime and commercial interests thought in terms of trade with the Far East, many westerners in the 1840s heard about the attractions of the Willamette Valley and stricken with Oregon fever hit the trail. Expansionists soon began asking for annexation and combined Oregon and Texas as issues in the election of 1844.

Candidate Polk could talk about all of Oregon, but President Polk had to be more circumspect. Soon after taking office Polk had Buchanan tell Richard Pakenham, the British minister, that the United States would compromise on the 49th parallel. When he did not hear from Britain, Polk withdrew his offer over the protest of Buchanan who feared war. The President assured his secretary that in dealing with Britain a nation had to be firm. Through the fall the President considered the Oregon problem, while editors at home and in England wrote about the threat of war. Many westerners yelled for all of Oregon at the time southerners and easterners favored compromise. Polk talked with Senator Thomas Hart Benton who thought that the 49th parallel would be acceptable; the President reminded him that Britain had rejected it. The men did agree that the United States should give notice of abrogating the Convention of 1827 and that settlers in Oregon should be covered by federal laws. San Francisco Bay, Polk told Benton, was as important as Oregon. When Congress convened in December, Polk asked for approval to end the agreement for joint occupation. While the pessimistic Buchanan thought war was near and called for "vigorous preparation," his chief showed how little he thought of the rumblings when he said the money would be well spent even if war did not come. Polk turned down a proposal to arbitrate because a question of limiting territorial expansion was too vital for submitting to outsiders. He could, however, compromise if Britain agreed to the 49th parallel and gave the United States a free port north of the line. Polk also said that he would talk with senators and might ask for "previous advice," that is, the Senate would agree to the compromise before it was formally submitted.

Congress was not in so big a hurry as Polk to abrogate the convention. In conversations with legislators, the President insisted that a firm and bold policy was the best way to keep the peace because Britain would take advantage of a faltering Congress and become more arrogant. To Congressman James Black he made the statement that became widely quoted about looking John Bull "straight in the eye." (Inasmuch as John stared right back as he made warlike sounds, Jonathan and John may be aptly described in the words of a later secretary of state as being "eyeball to eyeball.") The House agreed to giving notice in February, but the Senate deliberated until late April of 1846. Polk, always quick to assign ulterior motives to his opponents, complained that some senators thought in terms of 1848 rather than 49° or 54°40′; had they moved faster Britain would already have proposed a compromise. After the Senate sustained Polk in "the first great measure of my administration," he instructed Buchanan to address the notice to the queen, not the foreign secretary because heads of states dealt with each other.

The British cabinet quickly proposed a compromise with the 49th parallel as the boundary. Britain retained all of Vancouver Island, and the United States had its port in Puget Sound. Polk consulted his cabinet and found that Buchanan had become a 54°40′ man because true friends of the administration wanted all of Oregon; Polk said Buchanan had his eyes on the presidency. The country was at war with Mexico, so, as he seemed to have planned all along, he sent the papers to the Senate and asked for "previous advice" which he promptly received.

Most citizens accepted the Oregon settlement. Planters, many editors, and businessmen felt relieved because they had feared war with Britain, but extremists in the West thought they had been misled because they had supported other administration measures in expectation of reward. The British government faced problems at home that made the more cautious ministers favor compromise, although they may have been more grasping had they known about the war with Mexico in time. Polk, if his diary gives an accurate account, did not think in terms of war. Despite his campaign statements, he, as a skillful politician knew what was possible and when to compromise.

Since the 1830s, expansionists coveted Texas and California. Both Presidents Jackson and Tyler found the Mexicans hostile when they tried to acquire San Francisco Bay. Polk hoped to be more successful, but he faced complications. When Tyler interpreted Polk's election as a mandate for annexation of Texas and submitted the treaty to Congress, the Mexican government severed relations and prepared for war. Texans and Mexicans claimed the territory between the Nueces and the Rio Grande.

After the details of annexation were completed, Polk ordered troops commanded by General Zachary Taylor to occupy the land in dispute. Polk also inherited long-standing spoliation claims against Mexico. To solve the problems the President had to renew diplomatic relations, so he arranged for John Slidell to go to Mexico. Polk's secret instructions included offers to assume the claims in return for Mexico's accepting the Rio Grande as a western and southern boundary of Texas and to purchase California and New Mexico.

Political conditions were such that Mexican officials could not receive Slidell. While Polk fumed and awaited the return of his agent, tension mounted as opposing forces faced each other at Matamoros. In late April 1846, Polk told his cabinet that the United States tried to conciliate Mexico and had exercised forebearance. The time had come to be firm because all nations had to be treated alike whether weak or strong. Reports from General Taylor became more ominous. On May 9, the cabinet recommended that Polk ask Congress for a declaration of war when Taylor was attacked. A few hours later Polk received dispatches from Taylor who wrote that the Mexicans had fired on his troops. The president broke his no-work-on-Sunday rule to consult legislative leaders and prepare his war message. He stressed that American blood had been shed on American soil, but some representatives and senators who voted for war — 175 to 14 in the House and 40 to 2 in the Senate — called attention to the disputed blood-stained territory.

While most citizens supported the war effort, some Whigs and abolitionists called it "Mr. Polk's War" and a slaveowners' plot; by January 1848, they were strong enough to pass a resolution in the House by a vote of 85 to 81 that Polk had "unnecessarily and unconstitutionally" begun the war. Neither charge was true. Expansionists in all sections wanted war, and the President acted within the scope of his powers, although in the process he left himself open to criticism.

Polk had definite aims, and from his point of view he did not regard the war as one of conquest. The Texas boundary claims were legitimate. Mexico had not been able to pay the spoliation claims and would be unable to pay the indemnity the United States intended to demand when the war ended. Mexico did have California and New Mexico which the United States wanted. The President also had in mind making a token payment for the transfer of land. To achieve these aims — Taylor was not making much progress in northern Mexico — Polk decided to send an amphibious expedition under General Winfield Scott to land at Tampico and Vera Cruz. Meanwhile, Colonel Stephen W. Kearney and his column moved into the Southwest and had little trouble in establishing control over New Mexico before a small group of dragoons marched into California, where naval forces, a small expedition under John C. Fremont, and some civilians had overcome most resistance by January 1847.

Polk found himself with two senior generals who had monumental egos. Taylor, according to the President, did not have the ability to conduct a campaign; he personified the "Regular Soldier" who followed orders and assumed no responsibility. Taylor did not "prosecute the war with energy or vigor" and made a "great mistake" in granting an armistice after the battle of Monterrey. The President, after the press played up Taylor's successes, became convinced that the general had become "giddy" with thoughts of the presidency. Taylor, on the other hand, complained of ignorant people in Washington who interfered too much with his operations.

Scott, the senior major general, accepted command of the army two days after the declaration of war and within twenty-four hours convinced Polk that he was too "scientific and visionary"—just the opposite of Taylor. Like Taylor, Scott soon became too Whiggish for the President to trust. Polk, in discussions with Senator Benton, hit upon the idea of asking Congress to authorize him to appoint a lieutenant general for overall command. The man should be talented and resourceful, and Benton had the qualifications. As it turned out, Congress would not pass the law, and Polk complained from time to time that he had the responsibility of winning a war with generals in whom he had no confidence. In the meantime, the cabinet and Benton advised the President that Scott should command in Mexico because he was the ranking general. As a matter of "stern necessity and sense of public duty," Polk offered to let bygones be bygones, while Scott "almost shed tears" and reconsidered his earlier declaration that he did not want to face Mexican fire while people in Washington attacked his rear. The President, according to Scott, was "magnanimous." The truce was not long lasting. Before sailing from New Orleans, Scott leaked the plans for the attack on Vera Cruz to reporters.

Polk planned for peace while he planned for war. In the fall of 1846, he talked with Benton and other confidants about goals and about a commission, to be headed by Benton who always was available to negotiate a settlement at the proper time. For political reasons the President decided not to use a commission. Disappointed when the Mexican government did not sue for peace after the fall of Vera Cruz in March 1847, Polk decided to send a personal agent to travel with Scott and to open discussions with the enemy while the army fought its way to Mexico City. He chose Nicholas P. Trist, chief clerk in the State Department, who qualified as a Democrat by marriage to Jefferson's granddaughter and by brief service as Jackson's private secretary; he had served as consul in Havana and spoke fluent Spanish. Polk instructed Trist to get the Rio Grande as the boundary of Texas, Upper California (to include San Diego), New Mexico, right of passage across the Isthmus of Tehuantepec, and, if possible, Lower California. The United States would pay spoliation claims of American citizens and up to $30 million for the territory. On April 16, Trist departed on his secret mission, and Polk hoped that Whig editors, already guilty of "moral treason" for making political capital out of the war, would not get wind of it. Five days later, however, the President read two letters dated April 14 and 17 from anonymous special correspondents in the *New York Herald,* which gave details of Trist's mission. Polk became "more vexed and excited" than at any time since taking office. "Federal" editors and politicians, he declared, in their eagerness to embarrass the Democratic administration would send special messengers to Mexican officials. Buchanan could not account for the leak, but Polk suspected a "Whig clerk" whom he chewed out.

A clash of personalities marred the early relations of Scott and Trist, and Polk deplored the enmity between "these self important personages." In time, however, the diplomat and the general became friendly and cooperative, and Trist began discussions with Mexicans. In October 1847, Polk decided to recall Trist because he had made no progress and Mexicans should have no reason to think that the United States was anxious for peace. He would step up the war effort and assess Mexicans for the maintenance of the army. By the time Trist received orders to return to Washington he thought that he had made some headway; on the advice of Scott, the British minister, and Mexican officials, he decided to stay. Communications were slow, so Trist gained time by protesting his recall. Polk finally decided to have General William O. Butler send the recalcitrant home, but by that time Trist had obtained the President's minimum demands at a cost of only $15 million. Polk received the treaty of Guadalupe Hidalgo in February 1848, and after conferring with his cabinet and selected senators he decided to send the work of his "insubordinate and insolent" agent to the Senate where it was approved on March 10. For three years the President had grumbled about lazy bureaucrats who lacked initiative and sense of responsibility. Trist displayed these qualities in good measure, but Polk interpreted them differently and thought Trist was guilty of intriguing with Scott to embarrass him. As a result, the President showed his streak of vindictiveness by refusing to pay Trist's salary and expenses. In 1871, by special act of Congress, Trist received $14,599.

The war began with Polk's complaints about confidential and secret information getting into newspapers, and it ended on the same note. After the Senate approved the treaty, the *New York Herald* published letters and documents, which the President included with his message and which had been printed for the convenience of the senators. The "astonished" and "indignant" Polk bewailed the activities of "unprincipled letter-writers" (Washington reporters) while a committee investigated. A reporter named Nugent obtained the material but he would not tell from whom, and the Senate held him in contempt. Some people thought that Buchanan was the source of the leak, but Nugent cleared the secretary, much to Polk's relief.

Among the reform movements that disturbed the body politic after the 1820s, the anti-slavery issue came to be more and more dominant. The Founding Fathers, Polk maintained, recognized slavery when they worked out the compromises in the Constitution, and, furthermore, the Missouri Compromise of 1820 established an acceptable line of demarcation for the territories. He did not believe that slavery should be associated with his foreign policy and the war, but he found that many people did not agree with him. Soon after the war started Polk asked Congress for $2 million which he thought would be needed when he began peace negotiations. No Mexican leader could afford to yield to demands for territory without the backing of the army, and a prompt payment of $2 million would enable the unfortunate official to pay his troops and remain in power. The bill incorporating Polk's request had its ups and downs before final passage, and David Wilmot proposed his famous amendment to exclude slavery from territory acquired from Mexico. The President branded it as "mischievous and foolish." Polk, in conversations with Wilmot and others, pointed out that he had no desire to extend slavery; it was a domestic issue that had no place in a treaty which southern senators would not approve. Slavery, he believed, would not be profitable in California and New Mexico, so it should not become an issue. The President eventually received the money, the Wilmot Proviso was defeated, and the voices and tempers of extremists continued to rise.

In the summer of 1848, slavery became involved in the debates on territorial government for Oregon. The issue, Polk thought, posed the most serious threat to the Union since the Hartford Convention of 1814, and Congress could calm agitators by extending the Missouri Compromise line. The Oregon bill, however, excluded slavery, and the President approved it because it was north of 36° 30′. Characteristically, Polk charged the Whigs with using slavery in the presidential election while northern Democrats were timid. He, of course, wanted to "conciliate, as far as practicable, the North and the South." Demagogues endangered the Union as they made slavery a political issue.

Despite his success in acquiring the territory he wanted and in the face of controversies arising from it, Polk became interested in buying Cuba. Senator Stephen A. Douglas and John L. O'Sullivan, who coined the phrase "manifest destiny," called on him one day in May 1848 to talk about conditions in Cuba and suggested that he make Spain an offer. O'Sullivan professed to be in communication with Cuban revolutionaries who would welcome annexation. Polk found Lewis Cass, presidential aspirant, agreeable and brought the subject before his cabinet. Mason and Walker liked the idea, Buchanan and Marcy said it was not the right time, and Johnson wondered about having Spanish people in the Union. Only by "amicable purchase," Polk insisted, could the United States acquire Cuba, and he found that Spain did not want to sell. Six years later, in the administration of Franklin Pierce, Marcy was secretary of state, Mason was minister to France, and Buchanan was minister to Great Britain. They became involved in the Ostend Manifesto.

Meanwhile, in the White House, social life went on. James and Sarah Polk did not stint themselves as the First Family. Sarah, a gracious hostess, received callers on Tuesday and Friday evenings; not infrequently she dragged her protesting husband from his office to circulate among the guests. She entertained thirty or forty of her husband's dinner guests once or twice a week — although the President generally took credit for them when he confided to his diary, "I had a dining party on yesterday." Sarah also had to be prepared for numerous friends from Tennessee and for politicians who happened to be transacting business with the President when dinner was announced; they were invited to "take family dinner." To a caller who found her reading a book, Sarah explained that the author was coming to dinner, and she wanted to be able to talk with him.

In some ways Sarah seemed ambivalent as a hostess. She lived in Washington for the better part of a quarter of a century and knew her way around. She could exchange bon mots and witticisms with the likes of the urbane Henry Clay. She served liquors and wines, but she would not attend the race track. The Polks had a number of nieces and nephews who visited "Uncle and Aunt," but unlike the days of Jackson there

was no dancing for the young folks. Some people considered Sarah a bit formal, and this may be reflected in the family correspondence. Her nieces, nephews, and in-laws always referred to "Aunt Sarah" or "Sister Sarah." Only Samuel P. Walker regularly called her "Aunt Sally." Other correspondents called her "Mrs. Polk." To Old Hickory she was "Mrs. Poke"—unless a secretary corrected his spelling.

Polk found little time for recreation and relaxation other than his morning walks and infrequent horseback and buggy rides, but his confinement stemmed more from choice than necessity. He could comment in August 1846 that for the second time in seventeen months he had ventured outside the District of Columbia; he had visited Mt. Vernon earlier and this time he went to see Francis P. Blair who lived six miles out of town. When Congress adjourned, Polk spent four days at Fortress Monroe.

In late May 1847, Polk went on a nine-day trip via steamboat, rail, and carriage to Chapel Hill to deliver a commencement address. It was his first visit to the campus since his graduation in 1818. He mingled with the crowds and "never spent a more pleasant and delightful afternoon and evening" than he did visiting with old friends. Governor W.A. Graham showed a lack of respect by making a tardy courtesy call—but then he was a Whig. Later in the summer, the President, believing that he could maintain adequate communications with Washington, thanks to the "magnetic Telegraph," spent a fortnight in New England where the people received him with respect and cordiality. He declined Van Buren's invitation to visit because he thought it perfunctory; the former President had been offended when Polk ignored his advice on patronage and other matters.

Heartily rejoicing that Congress had adjourned and "exceedingly exhausted" by his "long confinement and great labour," Polk, in August 1848, boarded the "morning train of cars" for a ten-day respite at Bedford Springs, Pennsylvania. His entourage included only his navy surgeon, a servant, and his nephew, Samuel P. Walker. He transferred to a coach at Cumberland, Maryland, and was pleased when farmers gathered at way stations to greet him. At the springs he drank mineral water, chatted with guests, received callers from nearby towns, and marveled

---

A daguerreotype of President and Mrs. Polk made in the latter half of his presidential term. From Anson and Fanny Nelson, *Memorials of Sarah Childress Polk*.

at the speed of exchanging "telegraphic despatches." On the return journey the President decided to stop at Berkley Springs for the weekend. When he learned that the innkeeper had not reserved seats for his party in the coach that took guests to the railway station, Polk attributed it to the "low-bred" fellow's "vindictiveness in politics." The President refused an offer of some young men to give up their seats because he believed that when he was out of Washington he had no more privileges than other citizens. News of his embarrassment circulated through the community, and a Colonel Harmonson "procured a fine new coach" to take Polk to the train.

Polk's nightmares became realities when Whigs nominated and dissatisfied factions of Democrats helped to elect Zachary Taylor in 1848. Taylor, "wholly unqualified for the station," according to Polk, would be dominated by "designing men of the Federal party" bent on reversing "the whole policy of my administration," and the country would be the loser. In January, a cabinet member asked if Polk planned to attend Taylor's inauguration. He would, the President replied, if Taylor assigned him a place in the ceremonies; furthermore, if the President-elect came calling, he would be invited to dinner. Taylor did go to see Polk — they met for the first time — and returned several days later to dine with some forty guests that included Lewis Cass, Millard Fillmore, John Bell, Senator Jefferson Davis, and cabinet members. On Saturday, March 3, 1849, Polk cleared his "table" for the last time and left the White House. On Monday, Taylor and Polk rode together to the inaugural. On the return trip, the new President observed that "California and Oregon were too distant to become members of the Union and that it would be better for them to be an Independent government." Polk left "the well meaning old man" convinced that he was ignorant, uneducated, and of ordinary ability.

Polk was happy to be relieved of his "incessant labour . . . anxiety, and . . . great responsibility." He looked forward to becoming a "sovereign" instead of being a "servant." He and Sarah, accompanied by Robert J. Walker, took the "Southern route" — the long way around — on the homeward trip. They traveled by steamboat, train, ship, and carriage. Their itinerary included Richmond, Petersburg, Wilmington, Charles-

---

A copy of the portrait of Sarah Childress Polk, done by Healy during the Polk presidency. From Anson and Fanny Nelson, *Memorials of Sarah Childress Polk*.

ton, Savannah, Macon—where Walker left them because of illness—Columbus, Opelika, Mobile, New Orleans, Memphis, and many places in between. Although pleased by the receptions and friendly demonstrations, Polk found the dinners and ceremonies fatiguing. Rumors of cholera in Mobile and New Orleans frightened him, and he decided to forego the rich food at a banquet in favor of cornbread and ham which an obliging waiter provided. On the trip up the Mississippi River several deck passengers succumbed to cholera, and the already fearful Polk suffered a "derangement of stomach and bowels"—for years he had suffered with attacks of diarrhea—but he had no symptoms of the plague. He left the boat at Smithland, Kentucky, where he rested several days and a physician attended him. Cave Johnson and other friends rushed to his bedside. The Polks arrived in Nashville on April 2 to find their house in an "unfinished state," so they visited relatives in Columbia and Murfreesboro while workmen put on the finishing touches.

Anticipating retirement, the Polks bought Felix Grundy's home in 1847, and Sarah had gone down to inspect it and to order some remodelling. In the fall of 1848, she went to New York to buy furniture and arrange for its shipment to Nashville. After they moved into the house, which soon became famous as "Polk Place," James and Sarah kept busy arranging their books, papers, and other possessions, receiving well-wishers who called, and visiting friends. Polk suffered another attack of diarrhea brought on by his great fatigue and "emotional disturbances," which was probably complicated by "ulcerated colitis," and died June 15, 1849. Sarah managed her Mississippi plantation—she sold half of its 1,115 acres for $30,000 in 1860—and other property. She received the great and near-great, including Yankee generals, who passed through Nashville, and she enjoyed the role of grande dame for almost half a century.

Polk was one of the most successful occupants of the "President's House" and one of the least lovable. He more than compensated for his lack of brilliance by concentration and hard work—but how many Presidents have been truly brilliant? Polk's problems with an unpopular war and keeping diplomatic and military secrets make interesting comparisons with events of the 1960s and 1970s. As Polk's drive and ambition took him to political heights, far down the trail was his fellow Tennessean, Andrew Johnson, equally ambitious, tenacious, individualistic, and hard working. He, too, was a Jacksonian destined to be the third President of the United States from Tennessee.

4. Tennessee's Third President, Plebeian Andy

Among the thirty-nine Presidents of the United States, none had a more lowly beginning than Andrew Johnson, who clawed his way to the top rung of Democracy's ladder where the voices of men, instead of blending with those of a heavenly host on a dewey millennial morning as he had visualized in 1853, were heard throughout the land as they filled the air with recriminations and anathemas in an age of hate. In his vocation he rose from apprentice to master tailor; when he became a professional politician he served as alderman, state legislator, congressman, governor, senator, vice-president, and President. Johnson was born December 29, 1808, the second son of Jacob and Mary Johnson, who lived in the porter's cabin of Casso's Inn in Raleigh, North Carolina. Jacob, a ne'er do well, died in 1812 and left his poverty-stricken wife with eight-year-old William and Little Andy. Mary tried to keep her small family together and married Turner Daughtry, who was no better a breadwinner than her first husband. She apprenticed William to J.J. Selby, a tailor, and Andy when he was ten (some people say fourteen) followed suit. Andy learned to read while he developed digital dexterity with scissors, goose, needle, and thread. The apprentices found time for fishing, hunting, and mischief. One escapade involved Andy, William, and two friends who showed adolescent interest in Mrs. Wells's two "right smart" daughters by throwing rocks ("chucking") at her house, and Mrs. Wells threatened to prosecute them. Andy and William, already having trouble with Selby, decided to run away.

After two years of following their trade in several places and unable to reach an agreement with their former master, the Johnson boys, their mother, and stepfather loaded their possessions into a one-horse wagon and turned their faces westward. They arrived in Greeneville, Tennessee, on a September afternoon in 1826. Andrew liked the village of about 500 people; he and the Daughtrys decided to stay. William worked briefly as a carpenter and then moved on to Alabama and Georgia; he finally settled in Texas in 1857 without gathering any moss enroute. By May 1827, Andy had met, wooed, and married Eliza McCardle (1810–1876).

Eliza, daughter of an artisan, was as well educated as any girl in Greeneville; she had attended Rhea Academy. The Johnsons set up housekeeping in the backroom of the tailor shop; in the evenings Eliza taught her half literate husband to write, and she read aloud to him from books and government documents as he sewed. In contrast to Rachel Jackson and Sarah Polk, Eliza is a shadowy figure in the background—perhaps this results from her poor health and the paucity of family letters—but like Rachel she was unpretentious, practical, industrious, frugal, patient, and encouraged her husband. The young couple were good managers and soon bought a small house in which they lived until 1851 when they bought the large brick house on Main Street.

Andrew's family expanded as his business interests and political activities broadened. He took his parental duties seriously and encouraged his children, without too much success, to get an education. Each attended local academies. Martha, born in 1828, attended Miss English's Female Seminary in Georgetown in the mid-1840s when her father was in Congress. Charles, born in 1830, chose to remain at home and became part-owner of a drug firm; he was the family problem child and became an alcoholic. Mary, born in 1832, "went away to school" when she was eighteen; she attended Rogersville Female Academy about thirty miles from home. Robert, born in 1834, briefly attended Franklin College—a vocational school near Nashville; fear of cholera, if not acute nostalgia, caused him to return to Greeneville where he read law in the office of Sam Milligan or Robert McFarland. Andrew Junior, born in 1852, was called Frank and seemed to have been a family pet, which often is the fate of the last-born with grown brothers and sisters. During the hectic years of his father's presidency, Frank attended a private school in Georgetown.

Children of successful politicians seldom follow in their father's footsteps. Martha married David T. Patterson, close political friend of her

---

(*Above*): Main Street, Greeneville, Tennessee, circa 1875—the year of Andrew Johnson's death. Courtesy of Richard Harrison Doughty. (*Below*): Daguerreotypes of Andrew Johnson and his wife, Eliza McCardle Johnson. Courtesy Special Collections, University of Tennessee Library.

father, who became a judge and a United States senator. She served as
hostess in the White House because of her mother's illness. "We are,"
she is supposed to have explained, "plain people from the mountains of
Tennessee called here for a short time by a national calamity. I trust too
much will not be expected of us." Charles was commissioned as an assis-
tant surgeon in the Tenth Tennessee Infantry, U.S.A. — how he qualified
remains a mystery — and was killed near Nashville in a fall from his
horse in April 1863. Mary married Daniel Stover and lived on a farm
near Elizabethton. Robert helped manage the family property, served in
the state legislature on the eve of the war, received a colonel's commission, and raised the Fourth Tennessee Volunteer Infantry, U.S.A. He
served as his father's private secretary, 1865-69. Soon after the family
returned to Greeneville, Robert committed suicide for reasons not explained by biographers. Frank returned to Greeneville with his family,
married Bessie Rumbough in 1875, and died four years later.

The young tailor made friends easily, and his shop became a meeting
place, if not a hang-out, for young clerks, mechanics, and students from
two colleges nearby. Their more serious conversations dealt with politics, and the untutored Johnson learned from the collegians. In the local
debating society he learned to think and speak; he read history and
literature — not many books were available in Greeneville — for material
to embellish his speeches. Andy was intelligent, and he had more than
his share of intellectual curiosity. From the shop and the debating societies Johnson launched his political career in 1829 by becoming a successful candidate for alderman. For six years, sometimes as mayor, he performed his civic duties, expanded his business, sharpened his forensic
skills, and let his ambitions grow.

Elected to the legislature in 1835, Johnson worked hard, was punctual
in attendance, and "not unduly forward." He was neither fully committed to the Jacksonians nor was he an avowed Whig, although he favored
Hugh Lawson White for President. In the legislature he met a number
of men with whom he was to be associated for many years. He aroused
the Whigs back home, who favored internal improvements because he
opposed a charter for a railroad on the grounds that it was a monopoly.
While his enemies plotted against him, Johnson thought of retiring from
politics to make money. His retirement, however, was involuntary and
only temporary. Returning to Nashville in 1839, he flaunted his Democratic colors, opposed banks, and urged economy in state government;
the latter met the approval of Governor Polk. Johnson seized the opportunity to be a presidential elector in 1840 because he wanted to stump the

state for Van Buren and be recognized from Bristol to Memphis. The next spring Johnson advised Governor Polk on political conditions in East Tennessee and planned for a great turnout of Greene Countians when Polk campaigned in the area. Spurning the governor's suggestion that he run for Congress, Johnson won a seat in the state senate and helped Sam Milligan get elected state representative. Whigs put Lean Jimmy Jones in the gubernatorial chair and gained control of the lower house.

By the early 1840s Johnson had developed a style and an organization that he honed and expanded with the passing years. Behind every successful politician are friends who contribute to his rise. Some drop from sight for one reason or another, and rarely do they all last for the final hurrah. Andy was fortunate to have three friends who asked little and contributed a lot to his success. As young men, Sam Milligan, Blackston McDannel, William M. Lowry, and others met in the shop of A. Johnson, Tailor, where they discussed and debated topics of the day. They helped get out the voters when Andrew ran for alderman. They learned how to organize rallies, conventions, and meetings in the legislative and congressional districts and in the state when Johnson became a candidate for the General Assembly, for Congress, and for governor. They orchestrated the cheers, applause, groans, and jeers of the farmers, clerks, and mechanics who turned out to hear their plebeian champion always referring to his humble background and pointing out that Adam was the first tailor and Jesus was a carpenter. Andy effectively used anecdotes and a wit of sorts to spice his speeches. When face to face with opponents in debates, Johnson was ruthless and fearless because, as he put it, "the bullied party always occupies a losing position."

Johnson helped his friends as the opportunities arose. Milligan, a college graduate and an attorney, probably acted as Johnson's ghost writer before the war. He served in the General Assembly in the 1840s. Andrew appointed him to the state supreme court in 1864 and to the court of claims in Washington in 1868. Lowry was a merchant and wily political manipulator. When Whigs fired Lowry as postmaster in Greeneville, Johnson vowed to get revenge but advised his friend to be like Caesar and "adjust your robe and fall as decent as possible." Later Lowry became a federal marshal, but he did not ask for reappointment and moved to Georgia when the Civil War started. McDannel, the town plasterer and pension agent, could always depend on prompt bureaucratic response when he filed his clients' claims in Washington; he succeeded Lowry as marshal in East Tennessee.

State Senator Johnson, self-confident after two terms in the house and recognized as a full-fledged Democrat, became involved in affairs that attracted statewide attention. He showed that he was a good Jacksonian who believed in "hard money" and economy. He pricked Middle Tennesseans with a call for the capital to be moved to Knoxville. From time to time throughout his career Johnson, without batting an eye, presented novel and radical proposals that came to be called "andyjohnsonisms." Perhaps his first was a resolution for a committee to study "the expediency and constitutionality" of creating the "State of Frankland" to encompass East Tennessee and portions of Georgia, North Carolina, and Virginia. Another was a proposal for statewide election of congressmen. In 1841, the General Assembly was supposed to elect two United States senators. In times past this had been done in a joint session or "convention." Whigs had a majority of three in the house, while Democrats outnumbered their opponents 13 to 12 in the senate. Unable to compromise on a Whig and a Democrat, the Democratic senators—"The Immortal Thirteen" they were called—refused to meet in "convention." Sam Laughlin and Johnson were leaders in the fight while Polk advised from Columbia. Johnson argued that the two bodies were independent of each other, the practice of electing senators in joint session was wrong, and the time had come to correct the illegal custom. Not until October 1843, after the Whigs controlled both houses, were senators elected. By that time the voters of upper East Tennessee elected their Andy to Washington.

Johnson, driven by ambition, set his sights on higher office. During his legislative tour the Greeneville tailor formed a life-long friendship with George W. Jones of Lincoln County, a saddler by trade, with whom he served in both houses. One morning in February 1843, Johnson suggested some moves his fellow mechanic should make on "the chequer bord of politics." Andy successfully had used the tactics in the first district. By announcing his candidacy early he could discourage competition. He should press his claims on his friends and tell them that he wanted to serve them because "it will not do to be reserved in these days." By all means the nominating convention should be organized to reflect Democratic principles. About the same time Johnson informed Polk that Democrats in Greene and Hawkins counties were "completely organized" for the gubernatorial campaign that he expected Polk to win; as for himself, Andrew planned to be nominated for the lower house in Congress when Democrats met in convention.

As a member of the House of Representatives from 1843 to 1853,

Johnson generally supported Democratic measures on low tariffs, territorial expansion, banking, war, and slavery. All the while he displayed a disputatious and sometimes pugnacious independence that annoyed some of his colleagues who preferred more conformity. He conscientiously pressed the claims of his constituents and answered their letters. Without clerical help, he had to do his own research in preparing his speeches, which reflected the scope, however superficial his critics regarded them, of his studies. The homestead bill was his only proposal of national importance; he introduced it on March 27, 1846, and several times thereafter until his retirement from the House in 1853. He received more favorable comments from westerners and some eastern reformers than from southerners.

Johnson took the floor on many occasions to proclaim his views on issues of the day. Abolitionists, like New Englanders during the War of 1812, wanted to dissolve the Union; they trampled on the rights of states recognized in the Articles and the Constitution. As an expansionist, Andrew Johnson advocated the re-annexation of Texas, which he claimed was a part of the Louisiana Purchase, and he cited Emmerich von Vattel on international law. Johnson defended Polk's policies, but the President may not have approved being characterized as a "plebeian President," who, the congressman hoped, would give the country a "plebeian administration for once." Johnson wanted all of Oregon, and if the British lion growled, the American eagle would swoop from Mount St. Helens and drive the beast from the continent. The United States, according to Johnson, fought the Mexican War in self-defense. The conflict resulted from the action of Whigs who had been the first to introduce the bill for annexation of Texas, and they were guilty of prolonging the war by not supporting it. Andrew Johnson scorned those whose "bowels of compassion were moved" by the plight of Mexicans, while they forgot the sufferings of Americans imprisoned by the enemy. A war measure that Johnson opposed was the tariff on tea and coffee because it would fall most heavily on the laboring classes and weaken the Democratic party in the next elections.

Johnson established a reputation as tight fisted commoner. He favored longer workdays for government clerks and proposed a 20 percent cut in salary for those earning over $1,000 a year; at least he and Polk could agree that government clerks were lazy. The purchase of James Madison's papers would set a precedent for pensioning presidential widows. The Constitution, Johnson claimed, made no provision for the federal government to pay for paving the streets of Washington. The

Smithsonian Institution became a favorite target when the congressman was in an economizing mood, and in time of peace military appropriations received his attention.

Several times he introduced "andyjohnsonisms." His plan for rotation of federal employees stipulated that a clerk should not hold office more than eight years; each congressional district should have a quota of offices; and farmers and mechanics should have their fair share of jobs. To test the sincerity of congressmen who advocated internal improvements, Johnson asked for $500,000 for improving the Tennessee River — half to be spent on tributaries above Knoxville and the remainder on the river below. Perhaps he was in a puckish mood when he borrowed Thomas Hart Benton's and Andrew Jackson's old propositions for direct election of the president and senators.

Johnson and President Polk could agree on general Jacksonian principles, but in their detailed application the two men eventually found themselves at odds. As a young legislator, the tailor-turned-politician stayed within bounds and supported Polk. After the latter's second defeat in the governor's race and his own election to Congress, Johnson concluded that Polk could not regain his strength. While Polk maneuvered for the vice-presidential nomination in 1844, Johnson complained that his "ristless ambition" injured the party in Tennessee. Polk, furthermore, had shown no appreciation for the assistance Johnson had given him. As a result the congressman was not an ardent Polk supporter in Baltimore. After Polk moved into the White House their relations became less cordial. Johnson complained that he and George W. Jones had failed to get their share of patronage and Polk's appointments "all in all . . . are the most *damnable* set . . . ever made by any president." Why, Polk had appointed eight men from Columbia, one of whom took a Nashville whore instead of his wife to his job out West! Polk, according to Johnson, had not held the party together and *"was guilty of the black sin of ingratitude."* Just before the Democratic convention in 1848, Johnson feared that the President would try to get the nomination for a second term. To head off Polk, Johnson planted a story in the *New York Herald* that observers in Nashville believed Polk would run again.

Polk, for his part, disliked Johnson. While the congressman wrote that East Tennesseans could expect nothing from the President, Polk recorded in his diary that the "much agitated" Johnson had called for the first time in months. The congressman said that he had heard his opposition to the administration had been noticed, but he made no apology. Polk appreciated frankness and rejoined that Johnson and Jones had accused him of trying to coerce them, which was not true. Johnson departed with denials of opposing the President. Polk wrote that Johnson and Jones had been his enemies since 1839, and he would prefer two Whigs in their places. The President later took umbrage when a committee of which Johnson was chairman did not make a formal call to advise him that the House soon would adjourn. Polk commented on Johnson's presence at his last New Year's reception. The East Tennessean was "vindictive and perverse." The President concluded, "I am not aware that I have ever given him cause of offense."

Congressman Johnson frequently wrote to members of his family and to his friends in Greeneville, but only rarely did his earthy, country-boy humor show in his correspondence. He seemed less restrained with Blackston McDannel than with others. With apparent enjoyment he described the cloakroom version of the duel between William Lowndes Yancey and Thomas L. Clingman when the latter, thinking he was mortally wounded — Yancey had fired into the ground — stretched "his arams out like a pair of winding blades . . . not only made a copeous discharge of water, but . . . his Short bread came from him in great profusion." In another letter Johnson described a "*Kinder* of a 'bust'—not a big 'drunk'" that he and several friends had in Baltimore. They ate supper and attended the theater—"*Danseuses Vienneoises*" (a children's troupe)—after which they enjoyed oysters before retiring to their "virtuous couches." They arose at six, had a "drink," and arrived in Washington at nine "neither sick drunk nor groggy." When McDannel and Milligan fought in Mexico, Johnson passed on the hometown news about politics, the four schools that made Greeneville a center "for literature and profound learning," and "Scandal in abundance of al sorts." He added, "I presume a fair proportion of whoring is carried on by way of variety &c." Their families were well, and Milligan's "bethrothed" would "camly" wait for his return.

Johnson usually kept his woe and despair to himself, but one cold and cloudy day in January 1847, when his mood matched the weather, he unloaded on McDannel. The morning mail brought only bad news from home, and Johnson doubted that he had a friend in Greeneville. "I never," he exclaimed, "want to own another foot of dirt in the *damned* town while I live." He had no use for the "*god* for saken and hell deserving mony loving, hypocritical, back bighting, sundy praying scondrels of the town of Greeneville." He asked McDannel to "Send me some new fangled oathes so I can more effectually damn Some of that breed. . . ."

When time came for the decennial reapportionment, Whigs controlled the state legislature, and they gerrymandered Johnson's stronghold. Johnson decided that under *"proper circumstances"* he would consent to run for governor, and he requested the advice of David T. Patterson and Milligan. Johnson also suggested to another friend that East Tennessee Democrats had strong claims for providing the gubernatorial candidate which should be called to the attention of leaders in other parts of the state who could arrange for a "peoples candidate" to be presented to voters.

Johnson's friends were unable to organize the Democratic convention for a smooth nomination. Leaders in Middle and West Tennessee looked upon Andrew Johnson as a maverick who was a good Democrat only when he controlled the party. They preferred Andrew Ewing who had served in Congress with Johnson. Before the convention met, Ewing had agreed to support the East Tennessean. Several men were nominated including the two Andrews. Reminded of his promise Ewing withdrew his name. The other men dropped out and left the field to Johnson.

Whigs nominated Gustavus A. Henry, a prominent lawyer, a gentleman whose hortatory skills justified his sobriquet as the "Eagle Orator." Johnson overwhelmed him with his rough and tumble tactics. Because Henry had been a member of the legislature that gerrymandered the first district, Johnson told voters across the state that he had been "Henrymandered." When Henry proclaimed his love of the Irish in Memphis, Johnson produced a receipt for a contribution to Irish relief and asked to see his opponent's. The Whig press played up "The Immortal Thirteen," and Johnson's opposition to internal improvements. Andrew Johnson proclaimed himself to be "the man of the people and the people's man." He won with a majority of 2,250 votes; Democrats outnumbered Whigs 13 to 12 in the senate, but Whigs controlled the house, 44 to 31.

The new governor, like his predecessors, found himself restricted by the fundamental law and had to be satisfied with clerical and administrative chores. He began his term by declining an invitation to ride to the ceremonies with the out-going governor; he preferred to walk and mingle with the commonalty. Johnson's inaugural address was comparatively brief, but he rose to great heights as he identified himself with "progressive democracy" which he defined as a willingness to change when faced with new conditions. Democracy he described as a political ladder not unlike Jacob's spiritual ladder. The church and state ladders extended heavenward on converging lines and would meet somewhere in infinity and become one in heavenly bliss. Young men, meanwhile, could climb democracy's ladder and find a rung commensurate with their abilities. He was on more solid ground when he endorsed "judicious" internal improvements and called for homesteads. Whiggish editors did not let their readers forget the "Jacob's ladder" speech. Johnson mulled over problems that should be called to the attention of the legislators. In December 1853 he sent a message with recommendations for reducing the state's debt, financing public roads, liquidation of the Bank of Tennessee, special taxes for public education, and reform of judicial and prison systems. He also wanted endorsements for the homestead bill and constitutional amendments for direct election of senators and the President. The solons ignored most of the recommendations, but they did take an important step when they levied a poll tax of twenty-five cents and a small property tax to be used for public schools.

Johnson's bid for a second term involved him in a campaign that became as bitter as any in the annals of the state. By 1855, battered Whigs were disintegrating and in their stead rose the American or Know-Nothing party that appealed to xenophobes, protestant bigots, and 125 percent red-blooded Americans. Nashville, Clarksville, and Memphis had Know-Nothing mayors. Because of the secrecy of the party, the members did not hold a convention, but Meredith P. Gentry, one of the ablest men in the state, sent word from his "smiling farm with bubbling fountains" located in a "sequestered valley" to his neighborly editor in Shelbyville that he was a candidate. Democrats unanimously nominated Johnson without praising his record. Temperance advocates—"prohibitory voters" Johnson called them—tried to get the candidates to endorse a law for banning liquor sales; both refused. Gentry denounced Johnson's record in Congress and as governor. Andrew Johnson became the defender of freedom of the press, free speech, and freedom of religion. He blasted Gentry and Know-Nothings with invective and sarcasm as he defied them with a loaded pistol on the lectern. Johnson obtained copies of the secret oath and ritual of the Order of the Star Spangled Banner, which he read and pointed out that the members assembled from midnight until 4 A.M., "the hours at which bats retire to their hiding places and hyenas go forth in quest of dead bodies." Johnson won with 67,499 votes while Gentry polled 65,343. Democrats won only four of ten congressional seats and failed to get a majority in the legislature; obviously it was a personal victory for Andrew. His second term passed as had the first; with no veto and with little patronage, he attended to routine matters.

In 1856 and 1857, Johnson, never one to act hastily and without planning and whose "ristless ambition" rivaled that of any man to occupy the

White House, looked to his future. If he looked backward, he would have been satisfied with his progress. In less than thirty years he had climbed the rungs of democracy's ladder from tailor shop to alderman, to mayor, to state representative and senator, to congressman, and to governor. He had established a strong base among his homefolks; he had the support of the masses in his party; he had broken the Whig party and crushed Know-Nothings in the state; and he dominated his peers in the Democratic party.

Soon after the election, the governor divulged his plans. He had accomplished all he could in the state and the "true policy is to move upward and onward" and not stop in any place until people grew weary of him. Now was the time, if the next legislature was Democratic, for him to go to the Senate. He would wait until gubernatorial candidates manufactured "as much Senatorial Capital" for him as they could. His claims for the seat, Johnson reasoned, would be strengthened by vacating the governor's chair in favor of a new man. His plans worked out; in 1857, he stumped the state for Isham G. Harris and lined up support for himself. Tipped off about stratagems of Know-Nothings to defeat him, Johnson asked Lowry to go to Nashville when the legislature met. With a Democratic governor and a Democratic legislature, Andrew had no trouble moving up another rung.

Senator Johnson resumed his legislative career in December 1857. Still aggressive, blunt, and verbose in debate, literal in his interpretation of the Constitution, loyal to the little people for whom he thought he spoke, he became most concerned with national issues and preservation of the Union. His first official act, as might be expected, was to introduce a homestead bill. Ironically, Johnson eventually succeeded in getting his measure approved by both houses in the summer of 1860 only to have it vetoed by President Buchanan.

The senator continued to be a pinchpenny. He found nothing in the Constitution to justify appropriations for a transcontinental railroad or schools and an auxiliary police force in the District of Columbia. Johnson's comments on limiting the superintendent of the capitol to $10,000

(*Above*): Andrew Johnson's tailor shop in Greeneville with his brick residence in the background at the right. Courtesy of Richard Harrison Doughty. (*Below*): A drawing of the reception of foreign ministers by President Johnson shortly after becoming President. From Lloyd P. Stryker, *Andrew Johnson: A Study in Courage.*

for new furniture provoked Jefferson Davis, an old antagonist, to question his taste as an interior decorator, while another senator complained that he "wasted spirits and strength" of others. In remarks on the admission of Minnesota, Johnson called attention to the dangerous doctrine advocated by some colleagues whereby the federal government could prescribe qualifications of voters. It was an invasion of states' rights and violated the Constitution.

Johnson defended the South and its institutions. He was in his usual form when he spoke on resolutions to investigate John Brown's raid on Harper's Ferry. Reviewing the development of the slavery controversy, he declared that Jefferson did not have slaves in mind when he wrote the Declaration of Independence. Artisans and mechanics in the South earned higher wages than their counterparts in the North, and he cited statistics to prove it. He read gory details of Brown's activities in Kansas and described the suffering of the widows and orphans left behind. Brown was a murderer, thief, robber, and traitor. Brown's apologists — abolitionists, "modern fanatics" — "adopted John and his gallows as their Christ and their cross."

Someone discovered long ago that under the epidermis of a senator lies a thick dermis of presidential ambitions. In the case of Johnson, spots had been exposed as early as 1852 and more showed as the time came to select candidates in 1860. With feigned modesty and an outright lie, Johnson told a correspondent that he had not been and did not expect to be "an aspirant" for the presidency; neither he nor his friends were responsible for newspaper reports. Within weeks Lowry, Milligan, and Robert Johnson had organized the Greene County delegation to endorse the senator as a favorite son when Tennessee Democrats assembled in Nashville. From Washington, Johnson instructed Robert to be prudent and discreet in dealing with the supporters of Stephen A. Douglas; really he cared not "a fig" about the endorsement, but he could not dictate to his friends. Lowry on the Resolutions Committee, George W. Jones, and other adherents in caucuses and on the floor secured the long-sought approval of state Democrats without unduly antagonizing Douglas men. In preparation for the national convention in Charleston, Lowry wrote laudatory articles for publication in out-of-state papers and corresponded with Democrats in Minnesota and New York. Milligan passed out documents as he rode his circuit and congratulated Andy on the increasingly bright prospects that reflected the "spontaneous action of the people." Johnson recognized Douglas as the leading contender, but if Douglas faltered, a southerner should be nominated.

When Democrats, already badly divided on the wording of the platform, turned to nominating a candidate, Douglas could not get the necessary two-thirds majority. Johnson was never a serious challenger, but for thirty-six ballots his friends kept his name before the convention. He received only twelve votes — eleven from Tennessee and one from Minnesota. The senator may have used his favorite-son status as a gambit. He advised Robert on the eve of the convention to mix freely with delegates from the Northwest; if Tennessee yielded "first place" to Douglas, they would make a good impression and be in a position to ask for "first place" in 1864. Delegates from the Deep South walked out of the convention, but Tennesseans stayed on the advice of Johnson, Senator A.O.P. Nicholson, and two congressmen from West Tennessee. When Democrats gathered again in Baltimore, Johnson asked Milligan not to present his name; he wanted his friends to strive for unity and harmony in the party. The second effort resulted in two Democratic slates, Douglas versus John C. Breckinridge.

Senatorial duties kept Johnson in Washington much of the summer, and an illness, either real or one of convenience, confined him to Greeneville until late September. He eventually took the field to speak for Breckinridge. Johnson blamed the leaders, especially the ultras, for the split in the party. Southerners, he believed, should make their fight within the Union. After the election of Abraham Lincoln, the senator and some of his former Whig rivals held a big union meeting in Greeneville to endorse the Constitution, popular sovereignty, and property rights in slavery while they deplored sectionalism and asserted that Black Republicans enjoyed only a temporary success.

Returning to Washington in December, Johnson introduced constitutional amendments for direct election of the President and senators and several "unamendable" amendments for protecting slavery. On December 18 and 19, he made the most important, not necessarily the best, speech of his life. He was moderate and conciliatory as he pleaded with radicals on both sides. He thought that the southerners should stay in the Union where Democrats, if they remained united, controlled Congress and the Supreme Court. Lincoln was a minority President who could be defeated in 1864, and in the meantime the "middle states," including Tennessee, could keep the extremes united. The Union could be saved, Johnson believed, if northerners and southerners abided by the Constitution. Southern senators scowled, frowned, and taunted Johnson as he spoke. His speech made headlines, and he became, overnight, a traitor to the South and a hero in the North. Mobs hanged and burned his effigies in Memphis, Nashville, and other towns in Tennessee, while in Knoxville, Unionists thwarted demonstrators by the use of "clubs, pistols, and other implements of husbandry." So numerous were the requests for copies of the speech that Johnson ordered 10,000; Senator William H. Seward ordered 5,000; Senator Charles Sumner ordered 500; and other members of Congress ordered 100 copies each.

With the coming of the new year and as southern states seceded, Johnson frequently debated Jefferson Davis, Louis T. Wigfall, Joseph Lane, and others. The masses with their good sense and patriotism, Johnson believed, could see that anti-slavery laws violated the Constitution. If Democrats presented a united front in the Senate, they could defeat presidential appointments and control appropriations for the army and navy. Within the framework of the Union they could redress their wrongs. Massachusetts and South Carolina, Johnson declared, should be towed into the Atlantic Ocean to cool off, and the other states, North and South, could consider re-admitting them to the Union. Johnson concluded that southern leaders would not be satisfied with guarantees for slavery; they wanted control of a "monarchy" to put slavery beyond the reach of non-slaveowners. Tennesseans had little in common with the "Gulf States" and would be more comfortable in the Union if northerners recognized slavery. The senator attracted nationwide attention, and from the South came threatening letters. "Grand Junction" from the "State of Mississippi" warned that he intended to send his impudent mulatto slave armed *"with a Cowhide"* to leave *"marks of his attention"* on Johnson's back. Humiliated by his proximity to the senator, the slave, "Grand Junction" believed, would become obedient.

Johnson returned to Tennessee in the spring of 1861 where Unionists and Secessionists prepared for a second referendum to sever relations with the Federal government. The senator, no longer popular and hated by many people in Middle and West Tennessee, appealed only to East Tennesseans, and even some of them threatened him. Tennesseans voted in June by more than a majority of 2 to 1 to withdraw from the Union, but in East Tennessee 32,923 voters favored remaining in the Union while 14,780 preferred separation. Four days after the referendum, Johnson, urged by family and friends who feared for his life, left Greeneville in broad daylight and did not see his home again for eight years. Within a week he denounced "King" Harris and other conspirators who misled Tennesseans and explained his own stand to cheering audiences in Lexington and Cincinnati.

Back in Washington, Johnson, with Horace Maynard, a Know-

Nothing congressman from Knoxville, worked tirelessly to get aid for beleaguered East Tennesseans. For once in his life he found himself a hero with a following and a politician with influence in the White House. His bill for $2 million worth of arms for loyal citizens in seceded states sailed through both houses. He sponsored a resolution that emphasized defense of the Constitution and the Union as a war aim and disclaimed intent to overthrow established institutions. This he used later in Kentucky and elsewhere when he assured slaveowners they would not lose their property. In recognition of his bold stand and enhanced prestige, Johnson was appointed to the Joint Committee on the Conduct of the War. Lincoln had rewarded him earlier as patronage chief in Tennessee.

With the fall of Forts Henry and Donelson in February 1862 and General Albert Sidney Johnston's withdrawal from Middle and West Tennessee, President Lincoln started his experiment in governing conquered territory. Lincoln ignored a number of questions that could have been raised about the qualifications of Andrew Johnson for military governor of the state or it may be that the President thought Johnson's strong points far outweighed his weaknesses. At any rate on March 3, 1862, Johnson received his commission, which on its face gave him all the powers he needed. He followed the advice of General Don Carlos Buell and entered Nashville on March 12 without fanfare; Buell also warned him that the people would not welcome him. Several days later Johnson issued an appeal to the citizens of the state, and he tried to be conciliatory and to appear as a moderate. The governor appealed to their patriotism and pride as he invited them, regardless of their political preferences, to join him in his undertaking. The "erring and misguided" people should return to the fold because the war was fought in defense of the Constitution. "Treason in high places," he warned, would be punished.

Johnson found Nashville almost defenseless, and like anyone else in a similar position he concentrated on his problems and called for more and more aid, which Generals Henry W. Halleck and Buell could not meet. They resented his interference but tried to get along with him because of his influence in Washington. Lincoln finally admonished his governor, "Do you not my good friend percieve that what you ask is simply to put you in Command in the west. . . . You only wish to control in your localities, but this you must know may derange all other parts." When Confederate cavalry — as it did from time to time — threatened his enclave, the governor screamed for reinforcements and urged the mechanics of Nashville to stand up to the "proud aristocrats." Johnson also found time for a private feud with a captain on Buell's staff who refused to authorize payment of his telegraphic bills and countermanded an order for billeting the family of another officer. By direction of the secretary of war the captain rejoined the general at the front. Not until the autumn of 1863 did Johnson begin to feel secure and the Union army had some measure of control in the state. In the meantime, he began raising ten regiments for active duty.

Hundreds of Tennesseans fell into Yankee hands at Donelson, Henry, and Shiloh. Many of them believed that Johnson was sincere when he invited the "erring and misguided" to repent; they wrote letters of inquiry and declared that they had been misled or coerced into donning Confederate gray. The governor, with his long-held belief that aristocratic leaders lied to the people, had little trouble convincing himself that some of the boys deserved pardons. Johnson appointed Connally F. Trigg, a Unionist and Tennessean whom he recently had recommended as Federal district judge, to serve as a commissioner to visit the prisoners and identify the worthy poor.

If Johnson regretted his lack of executive power when he served as civil governor, he made up for it as military governor. Tennesseans, especially those in the Nashville area, did not understand at first the power of a military governor, but they quickly learned. He assessed wealthy southern sympathizers to care for the destitute wives and children of Confederate soldiers left in Nashville. The governor arrested three of the most prominent men in the area — William G. Harding, Washington Barrow, and Josephus C. Guild — for treason and had them confined in Fort Mackinac; he later protested when he heard that they were allowed to go at large in Detroit. When six prominent ministers in Nashville refused to take the oath of allegiance, Johnson arrested them as enemies of the state and shipped them to northern prisons. They not only used their pulpits to encourage rebellion, he said, but their influence was such that they changed "women and ladies to fanatics and fiends." Confederate cavalry and guerrilla bands raided so many towns and villages that the governor retaliated by arresting sympathizers and confiscating their property to repay loyal citizens for their losses.

Johnson's primary goal was to restore civil government as quickly as possible. Given the military conditions that prevailed in the state and the fact that a majority of Middle and West Tennesseans staunchly supported the Confederacy, the governor and the President, who were intelligent and experienced, should have recognized the troubles they would have. The generals did. Johnson had difficulties from the beginning.

The mayor and council of Nashville refused to take an oath of allegiance; the governor removed them from office. He ordered an election for circuit judge, then refused to sign his commission, and arrested him for his southern sympathies. The second man elected met the same fate. Johnson, well-guarded by Federal troops, made speeches in Nashville, Murfreesboro, and other nearby towns to rally the faithful. In his reports he appeared to have fooled himself and misinformed Lincoln because he greatly exaggerated the "union sympathy" that existed among the people. Prodded by Lincoln and with help from some old line Whigs, the governor organized a convention to call for restoring civil government, but the call went unheeded by the masses when Generals Nathan Bedford Forrest and John H. Morgan raided in Middle Tennessee. Forrest thwarted an attempt late in 1862 to elect congressmen from West Tennessee. In the summer of 1863, Emerson Etheridge and moderates started a movement to organize the state government, but Johnson did not think the time was right and Lincoln backed him.

Urged by Lincoln and with the amnesty proclamation and the 10 percent plan as guidelines, Johnson called a meeting of Unionists in January 1864, which began the year of the oaths in Tennessee. They endorsed resolutions, probably prepared by the governor, for a constitutional convention to abolish slavery and heard him declare, as he talked about restoring civil government, that the state had never been out of the Union — it had been temporarily paralyzed. A few days after the meeting adjourned, the governor, who thought restoration should begin on the local level, called for the election of county officials in early March. To qualify as voters, Tennesseans not only had to take the Lincoln oath "henceforth" to support the Constitution, but they had to "ardently desire" the defeat of Confederates and the success of the Union armies and to assist "loyal people" in achieving these ends. This was too much for many men who called the governor's addition the "damnesty" oath. Making it still more difficult, Horace Maynard, attorney general, stipulated that a six-months' residency for voters was required and it would begin the day that disloyal Tennesseans took the oath. This effectively kept them from the polls in March. Only a few people voted and showed that they were not ready for civil government.

In 1864, Lincoln sought re-election as President on the Union ticket to demonstrate that Republicans and Democrats supported the war effort. He chose Johnson as his running mate because the governor was a former Democrat from a border state and his loyalty to the Union was unquestioned. Johnson was well and favorably known to people in the

North, and his record as military governor was respectable. Johnson felt the pressure to make a good showing at the polls, and he wanted a functioning government before he left the state. He had no friends among the Secessionists, and he had alienated influential Unionists who thought that he was too radical. Some of these men found George B. McClellan and the peace plank in the Democratic platform quite attractive; Emerson Etheridge, in fact, denounced the Union candidates as despotic and infamous. Johnson moved to hamstring McClellan's supporters. The Union State Executive Committee called a meeting, and delegates — some self-appointed and some "soldiers" who could be relied upon — from forty counties met in Nashville. With Sam Milligan presiding, radicals refused to seat conservatives and proceeded to endorse Johnson's record, praised Lincoln, and called for the abolition of slavery. They prescribed the qualifications for voters which went beyond the amnesty and damnesty oaths. To cast ballots in the presidential election, voters had to swear to "cordially oppose" peace negotiations with "rebels in arms" and "heartily aid . . . loyal people in whatever measures" they adopted. Surely some war-weary Unionists labelled this the "goddamnesty" oath! William B. Bate, Balie Peyton, and other McClellan men withdrew the ticket after Lincoln turned down their appeal.

Johnson used the interval between election and inauguration to get a civil government in operation. Unionists called a meeting to select delegates for a constitutional convention, but General John B. Hood's invasion delayed it until January 7, 1865. Augmenting their numbers by inviting soldiers to join them, some 500 Unionists — William G. Brownlow arrived with 150 East Tennesseans half frozen by a long ride in box cars — gathered. After a bitter sectional squabble over representation apportioned to favor rabid loyalists in East Tennessee, they compromised on "one man, one vote" in return for conservative support of the "Parson" for governor and abolishing slavery. Sam Milligan proposed that the delegates draft constitutional amendments that would abolish slavery, void acts of the secessionist legislature, and authorize the military governor to order an election for civil officers. Conservatives objected that they could only select a general ticket for delegates who would revise the fundamental law. After three days of debate when conservatives were about to carry their point, Johnson, who had made a career of defending constitutions as he interpreted them, addressed the assemblage. Necessity and the inherent power of the people to alter their government spelled out in the state constitution, he argued, justified and legalized Milligan's proposals. The delegates resolved themselves into a constitu-

tional convention and rammed through the program. Johnson called a
referendum for February 22, and the amendments were ratified by a
vote of 25,293 to 48 which met the 10 percent requirement. Johnson proclaimed the amendments in effect, authorized the election of state officials for March 4, and departed for Washington on February 25, 1865.

The vice-president-elect, convalescing from typhoid fever, went to
Washington under protest because Lincoln insisted that he be present
for the ceremonies. Escorted by the retiring vice-president, Hannibal
Hamlin, the Tennessean complained of feeling weak and ill when he arrived at the capitol to take his oath. He requested a drink to settle his
stomach. Whether he had a shot, an "oversized" glass, or "three tum-
blers" of spirits is debatable, but the effects became embarrassingly ob-
vious to the cabinet members, senators, diplomats, and other members
of the audience in the crowded Senate chamber as Johnson delivered a
rambling speech. Newspapers played up the spectacle and, as his popu-
larity declined during the next four years, his enemies made the most of
it. In fact, Johnson was a moderate drinker who did not get drunk. Lincoln admitted that his vice-president made a "bad slip" but declared,
"Andy ain't a drunkard." Johnson became a house guest of the Blairs,
his friends since the days of Jackson, in Silver Springs where he regained
his health and his poise.

Six weeks after the inauguration Lincoln was assassinated and Andrew Johnson became President of the United States. He began his administration about as well prepared by his political experience as any of
his peers and better prepared than a number of them. He had ability and
a good mind. Whether he was as well endowed with a temperament to
serve in such chaotic times has been a subject long debated. Fortunately,
from the presidential point of view, Congress was not in session. While
representatives, senators, reporters, editors, and the public sized him up
and speculated on the indigence and punishment he had promised traitors, the President moved his family—children, grandchildren, and in-
laws—into the White House after Mary Lincoln finally vacated it. Johnson, a good administrator, had a well-organized staff in contrast to the
casual Lincoln. He began his day about 6 A.M., read newspapers, break-
fasted at 7:30, and went to his office. He, like his predecessors, tried to
make himself accessible to callers of high and low estate—and he had
hundreds who sought pardons. He dined about four in the afternoon
and returned to his office to work until eleven. Johnson did not care for
the theater or society, but his daughter, Martha Patterson, maintained
the standards of presidential hospitality. The President, even in time of

trouble, took his grandchildren to parks and often, in the company of his bodyguards, drove in the country.

Although domestic problems required almost constant attention, used most of his energy, and exhausted his patience, Johnson with Secretary of State William H. Seward had some success in foreign affairs. During his administration the United States added to its territory by the purchase of Alaska. He restrained his bellicose generals—Ulysses S. Grant and Phil Sheridan, who wanted to help Benito Juarez—and he called on Napoleon III to withdraw troops from Mexico. The President suppressed Irish nationalists who used bases in the United States from which to make raids across the Canadian border and annoy the British. Anson Burlingame, minister to China, won friends for the United States in the Far East. Reverdy Johnson, minister to Great Britain, reached an agreement to arbitrate disputes arising from the Civil War, only to have the Senate reject it. In his last annual message, Johnson gave some attention to Cuba and indicated that the United States might become involved in its problems; he took advantage of the opportunity to say that the army of occupation in the southern states did not set a good example for Latin Americans.

President Lincoln had clashed with Republicans in Congress over the conduct of the war and reconstruction. Radical abolitionists not only wanted to end slavery but called for Negro equality; they joined more moderate party members who resented Lincoln's loose interpretation of executive powers. With finesse, patience, and flexibility, Lincoln had avoided an open rupture between the two branches of government; nevertheless, they were on a collision course in April 1865. Johnson's words and actions as senator and military governor resulted in the Radicals' welcoming him as President. Preservation of the Union, Johnson maintained in 1861, was the war aim, and he assured people in the border states that slavery would not be abolished; later he was to accept abolition as a second goal. His attitude toward equality for blacks was that of contemporary southerners and many northerners; Negroes were inferior.

While Radicals, Conservatives, and Democrats jostled each other in the waiting room, Johnson politely received individuals and groups in his office, listened attentively to their advice and pleas, and then followed his own course. Unencumbered by personal responsibility he had

---

A Currier and Ives print of Johnson as President. Courtesy Special Collections, University of Tennessee Library.

blustered for four years about the punishment to be inflicted on traitors. He found, however, that sitting in the presidential chair gave him other points of view. He concluded that he should exercise leniency and get the southern states back into the Union as rapidly as possible. Johnson took advantage of the congressional recess to continue, with a few changes, Lincoln's plan of reconstruction—"restoration" he called it. By December, all of the seceding states, except Texas, met the requirements and had elected members of Congress. During the process Johnson, as had Lincoln, recommended the enfranchisement of literate and property-owning Negroes; unfortunately none of the states followed this advice. Some of the new legislatures moved in the other direction with black codes, based in part on the vagrancy laws of northern states, to regulate the newly freed labor force. Then as another affront—in the minds of victorious Yankees—southern voters looked to their old leaders and returned many of them to Washington.

When Congress reconvened in December 1865, the various factions served notice on Johnson that they intended to have a voice in reshaping the South by creating a joint committee on reconstruction. Both houses refused to seat recently elected southerners. The President presented his annual message which contained his ideas expressed in the polished prose of George Bancroft, the historian. (Johnson, aware of his literary shortcomings, used ghost writers, usually the members of his cabinet.) He argued that southern states had not seceded but had suspended their functions and could be restored by ratifying the Thirteenth Amendment and reorganizing their governments. This they had done, he contended, so the southern states should be recognized, their representatives and senators should be seated, the troops should be withdrawn, and their people should be returned to peacetime pursuits. As for Negro suffrage, Johnson said, he found nothing in the Constitution to authorize the creation of a new class of electors by agents of the Federal government—states determined the qualifications of their voters. The President was not belligerent, and Radicals such as Thad Stevens and Charles Sumner, not to mention more conservative men, were wary about challenging him.

Relations between President and Congress became strained early in 1866 and open warfare erupted before the end of the year. Lyman Trumbull of Illinois, a moderate, introduced and both houses approved a bill extending the life of the Freedmen's Bureau, whose agents were hated in the South. Johnson surprised the moderates with a veto in which he declared that the agency was not needed in time of peace; the bureau invaded precincts of civil government and provided for trials without juries, from which there were no appeals; and the Constitution did not authorize the support of indigents. The measure applied to states not represented in Congress at the time of its passage. On Washington's Birthday a cheering crowd assembled in front of the White House and called on Johnson for a speech. He made one of his stump speeches in which he denounced old southern leaders, whom he compared with the Radicals now trying to destroy the Union. When called upon to identify the latter, the President unwisely mentioned Stevens, Sumner, and Wendell Phillips. In March, the Civil Rights Act, which Republicans considered mild and southerners thought was radical, arrived on Johnson's desk. Ignoring the advice of moderates and members of his cabinet, he vetoed it because eleven states were not represented in Congress; the bill discriminated against immigrants and encroached on the rights of states. Johnson followed this with another intemperate address to a delegation of soldiers and sailors. He began using his patronage powers but not adroitly, and he alienated more moderates. As a result, Congress overrode the veto, and the President lost the initiative.

Other developments contributed to the break between President and Congress. Afraid of losing control of the Federal government as southerners demonstrated their opposition to reconstruction and especially Negro suffrage, Republicans — Conservatives and Radicals — strengthened their position by submitting the Fourteenth Amendment (primarily designed to safeguard civil rights of Negroes, to reduce congressional representation of states that imposed restrictions on voters, and to prohibit southerners who served the Confederacy from holding political office unless pardoned by Congress) and stipulating that the conquered provinces had to ratify it as one of the steps toward readmission. They also thought that it would pave the way for blacks voting in the North. Uncertain of their ability to override Johnson's vetoes, the Republicans made a concerted effort to increase their strength in Congress in the off-year elections. While editors propagandized, politicians waved the bloody shirt and exhorted the faithful to vote as they had shot during the war. The President's friends tried to form a coalition by calling the National Union Convention to meet in Philadelphia where Democrats from the North and South joined with a few Conservative Republicans.

Johnson, clinging to his principle that well-informed masses could distinguish between right and wrong, made his famous swing around the circle that took him into the major cities in the North to tell the people how Radicals subverted the Constitution and intended to alter the government. Times had changed since his successes on the stump in the

1850s and his wartime speeches before friendly audiences; his listeners still harbored their hatred for the South, and they believed the reckless charges of the Radicals that the fruits of victory—especially political power—would be lost if the "dipsomaniacal charlatan" had his way. Johnson could not resist bandying words with hecklers planted in the crowds. Candidates for governor or Congress could make good impressions on their audiences by exchanging insults, but the President of the United States cheapened the high office—so his enemies and some of his friends said. Northern voters believed the newspapers and the Radicals and sent more Republicans to Congress, but they did not change Johnson who held tenaciously to his interpretations of the Constitution and his belief in the common sense of the common man.

With enough Republicans in Congress to override vetoes, Stevens, Sumner, and Company proceeded to indoctrinate as many as possible of their Conservative colleagues. Their Reconstruction Act of March 1867 established congressional and military control of the southern states, and the Radicals strengthened it with supplemental acts from time to time when the President and former Rebs found loopholes. The Radicals, beginning to distrust the Supreme Court, also reduced the number of justices to seven before Johnson could fill three vacancies. The Radicals enfranchised Negroes in the District of Columbia. The Tenure of Office Act, Radicals thought, restricted Johnson's control of his cabinet appointments and protected Secretary of War Edwin M. Stanton, who served as their spy in the White House. The President used carefully reasoned—he had well-qualified advisers—constitutional arguments in his vetoes of these and other measures which Congress overrode with ease.

Johnson's restoration policy caused Radicals to question his sincerity and motives soon after he took office, and they talked about impeachment. His vetoes of the Freedmen's Bureau and Civil Rights acts and swing around the circle resulted in more talk and threats. The vetoes in 1867 prompted several congressmen to propose impeachment. Their flimsy charges could not be sustained, so committees looked for additional evidence. In the summer of 1867, Johnson removed Generals Phil Sheridan and Daniel Sickles, who had followed a hard line in their military districts. Long suspicious of Stanton, the President had exercised considerable patience and retained him in the cabinet. When he learned that the secretary had withheld information about the New Orleans riot (blacks versus whites) and the court's recommendation of clemency for Mary Surrat, who had been hanged for her alleged role in the plot to assassinate Lincoln, Johnson suspended him and gave General Grant the temporary appointment. The latter agreed, so the President thought, that he would not turn the office over to Stanton if the Senate failed to approve his action. Already angry with Johnson, Radicals became concerned about their political power when Northern Democrats in 1867 showed surprising strength in state elections and voters in Minnesota and Kansas turned down Negro suffrage. The results seemed to sustain the President's claim that the people supported him and were tired of Reconstruction.

Radicals and Johnson rapidly moved toward a showdown. When Congress met in December 1867, the President, as required by the Tenure of Office Act, sent word that he had suspended Stanton; in the middle of January, the Senate did not concur with his reasons. Grant, contrary to his agreement with Johnson, turned the office over to Stanton. On February 21, the President fired Stanton and appointed General Lorenzo Thomas. Stanton refused to be fired and took up residence in his office. Congress was in an uproar, and three days later the House voted to impeach Johnson for high crimes and misdemeanors. The allegations revolved around violation of the Tenure of Office Act and criticisms of Congress. The real reason for impeachment was the struggle for political power. Radicals and many Conservatives wanted to carry through their political and economic designs, and thereby make the Republican party supreme for years to come. If they convicted Johnson, they would set a precedent and subordinate future executives to the legislative branch and effectively change the constitutional system to a form of government resembling the parliamentary system of Great Britain; Presidents would become congressional puppets. The idea was implicit in the Reconstruction Act of 1867, the Tenure of Office Act, and in the Army Appropriations Act which effectively prevented the President from being commander-in-chief by the appointment of a lieutenant general who would be protected by Congress.

From March 30 to May 16, 1868, the Senate heard witnesses and the arguments of the House managers and Johnson's counsel, while Chief Justice Salmon P. Chase struggled to maintain some semblance of fairness in the proceedings. The President's attorneys—among the best in the nation—took charge of their belligerent client, and they forbade his taking the stand in his own defense, would not let him visit the Senate chamber, and ordered him not to talk with reporters. Johnson carried on his usual activities and maintained an outward calm, but he spent some sleepless nights pacing the halls. They did not have to prove, the managers argued, that the President violated any laws; his denigrations of

Congress and his attempts to circumvent the Reconstruction Acts were sufficient. In reply, counsel for the defense maintained that Johnson had violated no law because Stanton did not come under the Tenure of Office Act and the President could challenge that law to get it into the courts. Johnson had not conspired to violate a law, and his criticisms of Congress came under the right of free speech. When the Senate voted on the articles, seven Conservatives joined twelve Democrats to deny the Radicals the necessary two-thirds majority needed for conviction. They saved the independence of the presidency and set a precedent that political differences between the executive and legislative branches were insufficient grounds for impeachment. Congress, nevertheless, called the tune for the remainder of Johnson's term.

The President used his last annual message as an opportunity for a parting shot at Congress. The Reconstruction Acts, he suggested, had failed after a fair trial. Curtailment of the executive's powers as commander-in-chief and the Tenure of Office Act were unconstitutional. As an admission of error, Congress should repeal these laws and thereby gratify patriotic and intelligent citizens. Johnson recommended legislation or an amendment to exclude members of Congress from consideration when a vacancy occurred in the presidency or vice-presidency. He dusted off his old proposals for direct election of the President and senators and limited terms for federal judges. As a last "andyjohnsonism," his recommendation for handling the national debt led to the charge that he favored repudiation. Soon thereafter Johnson, who had been generous with pardons, cleared the list of former Confederates—including Jefferson Davis—accused of treason.

In the closing weeks of his administration Johnson wound up his affairs. On March 4, 1869, Grant rode alone to his inauguration because he refused to share his carriage with the out-going President. On the other hand, Johnson refused to ride with the man he called a faithless liar and worked in his office, surrounded by his cabinet, until about noon. The Johnsons were guests in the home of John Coyle, editor of the *National Intelligencer,* for almost two weeks. They bought new furniture for their home in Greeneville, which had to be restored after being used for a hospital and quarters by Yanks and Rebs when they were in the vicinity. The people turned out to greet the homeward bound

A ticket to the impeachment trial of President Johnson, 1868. Courtesy Special Collections, University of Tennessee Library.

Andy Johnson they once cursed; he had tried, they thought, to abate the horrors of Reconstruction.

Johnson retired from office as a fairly well-to-do man. Unlike Jackson and Polk, Johnson managed his personal finances so he could live modestly but comfortably within his income; he invested wisely and was a creditor instead of a debtor. As a young and skilled "mechanic," he pleased his customers and in time employed apprentices and journeymen. He bartered his services for farm commodities which he sold to merchants, and he made clothes for them to carry in stock. As a poor boy, Johnson knew what it was to be destitute, and as a young adult he tried to have an emergency fund. During an initiation ceremony, so a story goes, when he was supposed to have divested himself of all coins, Johnson was called upon to produce a bit of metal. He startled his conductor by producing a $20 gold piece from a secret hiding place in his underwear. Johnson began buying small parcels of land and lots at sheriffs' sales. With his business expanding he became a money lender. He started out as a legislator denouncing railroads as monopolies, but in 1858 he held over $13,000 worth of railroad bonds. Also, in the 1850s, he invested regularly in treasury notes. In 1872, he deeded to his daughter Martha a 513-acre farm that he had received in payment of a debt. When the First National Bank of Washington failed during the panic of 1873, Johnson had $73,000 on deposit; he collected 60 percent of it before he died, and his heirs received the remainder. His estate was estimated to be between $150,000 and $200,000, which should have been a satisfying accomplishment for the penniless tailor turned politician. In the process of acquiring his fortune, be it said, he was accused of many crimes but not of stealing.

Back in Greeneville, the former President looked after his affairs and renewed friendships. He accepted invitations to visit Memphis, Chattanooga, Murfreesboro, and Nashville. Johnson had been a professional politician for over thirty years and could not remain passive. Furthermore, he was driven by a desire for vindication and revenge and wanted to return to Washington as an elected official. State legislators turned down his bid for the Senate in 1869, when, according to one story, a friend paid $1,000 each for the two votes needed for his election, but Johnson refused to be elected in that fashion. In 1872, he met defeat

---

(*Above*): Johnson's home in Greeneville in the 1850s. (*Below*): A scene from Johnson's funeral in Greeneville, 1875. Both photographs courtesy of Richard Harrison Doughty.

when he ran for congressman-at-large. He used these occasions to mend his fences, however. In January 1875, the legislators required 55 ballots to choose "Parson" Brownlow's successor. The "Parson" and Andy Johnson had fought each other as Whig and Democrat; they had agreed on staying in the Union in 1861; they parted company on Reconstruction. Brownlow had replaced Senator David T. Patterson, Johnson's son-in-law, in 1869. Now Johnson could gloat over his opportunity to replace Brownlow.

The old plebeian's luck held out. Under normal conditions he would not have gone to Washington for almost a year, but Grant called a special session on March 4. When the new senator went to Washington, some editors hailed his return; contrasted with Grant, Johnson became an honest giant. A visitor suggested that his two rooms in the Willard Hotel were not so large as those he once occupied up the street, but the former President allowed as how they were more comfortable. Johnson allegedly promised Republican legislators in Tennessee not to attack Grant; if he made such a commitment, he could not resist temptation once he took his seat. For two weeks the senator did his homework, and then in the crowded chamber he denounced Grant's handling of Reconstruction in Louisiana, his desire for a third term, and his acceptance of expensive gifts; he warned the people that he could foresee the loss of freedom in the "stratocracy" their enemies prepared for them. Congress adjourned two days later. On July 31, 1875, Johnson died of a stroke while visiting in the home of his daughter in Carter County. Of the old tailor shop gang, only Blackston McDannel was around to act as a pall bearer.

Andrew Johnson generally receives low marks as a President, and some critics argue that he brought most of his troubles on himself because of his stubborn refusal to seek compromises with the more moderate Republicans. It takes two to compromise, and enough moderates may not have been able to go contrary to the opinions of their constituents whose wartime passions had not cooled and the businessmen who wanted more favors from a pliable Republican party. Then, too, southerners did not always follow Johnson's advice. Andy labored under a major handicap because of the way he became President—he was not the leader of any party or faction. Johnson does deserve credit for the courage with which he faced his opponents and preserved the independence of the presidency. Now he may be compared and contrasted with his fellow Tennesseans who traveled the same paths and roads that led to the White House and faced some of the same issues and problems enroute.

5. Comparisons and Contrasts

Jackson, Polk, and Johnson were alike in many ways, yet each was a strong individualist who responded to the changing times in his own way. Highly intelligent and well-informed men, they were pragmatic in their approach to the problems they faced. Of the three, Jackson possessed the best mind. Each man was honest in handling his personal finances; Johnson as military governor of Tennessee could have stolen a fortune had he wished. Each was a strong family man. Andrew Jackson Junior and the Johnson boys did not live up to the expectations of their parents; Martha Johnson Patterson, however, was a source of strength for her father. Rachel Jackson managed the farm, if not her husband who was away from home so much of the time. Sarah Polk, constantly at her husband's side, contributed greatly to his successful career. Jackson and Johnson enjoyed relaxing with the children and adults in the family circle, but Polk probably never completely relaxed even with Sarah and Cave Johnson.

Politicians should have tough hides that render them comparatively safe from the shafts hurled by opponents and impervious to the needling of critics. They seldom do, however, and the three Tennesseans particularly had thin skins. Jackson early in his career became well known for his short temper; with age he learned to control and use it to his advantage through intimidation of his enemies. Polk learned self-discipline as a young man and rarely let himself go in a healthy outburst of rage, but when he was sorely vexed he lowered his blood pressure by recording his feelings in his diary in chaste prose. Johnson, in spite of his financial and political successes, remained sensitive about his lowly origins, whereas Jackson overcame his feelings of inferiority — some people say that he overcompensated. Johnson's opponents in the House and Senate took advantage of his weakness during debates; on the other hand, Johnson, the vote-seeker, made the most of expanding democracy and never let his audiences forget that he was a mechanic who labored with his hands. Jackson, Polk, and Johnson interpreted opposition to their policies in terms of personal enmity, but other Presidents have done the same—perhaps it is a presidential trait if not an occupational disease.

Basically, Tennessee's three Presidents were Jeffersonian Republicans who believed in low tariffs, economy in government, states' rights, and the ability of the so-called common man to make the right political decisions when fully informed by his leaders and newspapers. When Jackson entered the presidential list in the 1820s, he had not been a candidate for office for two decades and could not be considered a party man. He found the Republicans, in the absence of Federalist opposition, split among strong factions led by Adams, Clay, Calhoun, and Crawford. Jackson's strength lay in his being a national hero hailed by the masses as one of their own, and he took advantage of it. With the able assistance of Van Buren, Francis Blair, Amos Kendall, and others, Jackson refashioned the party. His influence was such that historians used his name to identify an age, and later generations of Democratic politicians installed him in their pantheon.

Polk and Johnson, in contrast to Jackson, were politicians who made careers of holding elective offices; they worked from bases that started in their home counties, grew to include safe congressional districts, and then encompassed the state. In the days when voters held oratorical prowess in high regard, Polk and Johnson successfully used facts, reason, and aggressiveness. Congressman Polk followed Jacksonian policy and became recognized as Jackson's man in the House. As speaker and later as President, Polk with considerable success kept the Democrats in line and set precedents that his successors expanded. Johnson, on the other hand, was prone to go his own way in the party unless he stood to gain thereby or was the man calling the signals.

Jackson, Polk, and Johnson displayed physical and moral courage. Jackson and Johnson confronted and faced down armed opponents; the former shot down several. They spoke out on issues of the day and created a few of their own as they attempted to bring about changes that they thought were needed. None of the triumvirate shrank from responsibility; on the contrary, according to their critics, they lusted for power.

The three Presidents defended states' rights up to a point. Jackson distinguished between states' rights and nullification and prepared to use

A sketch of Jackson in his first year as President. From John Frost, *Pictorial Biography of Andrew Jackson.*

force in South Carolina. Johnson chose the Union when the break came in 1861. Polk faced no comparable crisis.

Jackson established a record that resulted in his being classified among the great. He was an able administrator who shook up the bureaucracy with his ideas on rotation in office. He conferred regularly with his cabinet, party leaders, and members of Congress to get his policies enacted into law and his vetoes sustained. Jackson was successful in his conduct of foreign affairs. He defeated the powerful elite when he destroyed the Bank of the United States. Jackson and his cohorts used Blair's *Globe* and other party organs to mold public opinion. In the process of selecting his successor Jackson wrecked the Democratic party in Tennessee. He had a sense of history and understood the significance of his actions. In October 1833, the President sent Andrew Junior a newspaper that carried his memorandum on the bank with instructions to file and preserve it because "the history of my administration will be read with interest years after I am dead, and I trust will be the means of perpetuating our happy Union and our liberties with it."

Polk, reticent, reserved, designing, colorless, and with few if any endearing personal characteristics, was one of the most successful of the thirty-nine Presidents to date. He went into office with four major objectives which he attained. He was an able administrator albeit he paid too much attention to minutiae. Polk knew how to use the *Union* and other newspapers in molding public opinion. He worked closely with members of Congress in getting needed legislation. As chief of state, Polk complained bitterly about wasting his time on amenities, but he conformed to protocol. In foreign relations Polk reached his goals; he handled Great Britain with aplomb while others lost their nerve.

As commander-in-chief, Polk carefully supervised, perhaps too closely supervised given the poor communications and distance involved, military affairs in Mexico. He became positively paranoid about Generals Taylor and Scott, but, considering the proclivities and personalities of his generals, perhaps he had good reasons to be suspicious. During the course of the war Polk was bedeviled by garrulous politicians, officers, and clerks who leaked diplomatic and military secrets, including plans of future operations, to the press. The Mexican War, like the involvement in Vietnam in the 1960s, became unpopular. Had Lyndon Johnson

---

The Johnson tailor shop in Greeneville draped in crepe either upon the death of Johnson or for a Fourth of July celebration. Courtesy of Richard Harrison Doughty.

read Polk's diary he could have found solace but not answers to his problems. Polk, too, had a sense of history—it may have been the habit of a lawyer or a manifestation of his mean, vengeful streak—that caused him to record in his diary the details of his quarrel with a congressman so that "others who may come after me may have occasion to refer to the facts, as they are known to me to exist."

Johnson, always an outsider, climbed democracy's ladder and in the process became a more successful leader in Tennessee than either Jackson or Polk as he served two gubernatorial terms and went to the Senate. He took a forthright stand on secession and found himself in the unaccustomed role of hero in the North and an outcast in the South. He failed to achieve his goals as military governor, but other men probably could have done no better. Elected to the vice-presidency on a coalition ticket of Lincoln's making and entering the White House through a side door, he was a President without a party; he was still an outsider regarded with suspicion by congressmen, businessmen, and the general public. In carrying out his plans of Reconstruction he clashed with the Radicals and then alienated Conservatives. Johnson was inflexible and dogmatic in his interpretation of the Constitution. He was right, and right, Johnson maintained, should not be subordinated to wrong to achieve a compromise. Johnson's opponents thought that they were right, and they were just as dogmatic and inflexible as the President. Johnson failed to put together a new party at the Philadelphia convention. He failed to get public opinion on his side in 1866 and later. He lost the support of friendly newspapers as his fight with Congress progressed. He did use his position as commander-in-chief in reconstructing the South until Radicals rounded up the votes to override his vetoes and implement their plan of Reconstruction. Johnson did have some success in foreign affairs, and he was a good administrator. Johnson, his attorneys, and the nineteen senators who voted for his acquittal deserve the credit and the praise for maintaining the independence of the executive branch of the federal government.

They were three Tennessee Democrats who prospered because of their innate intelligence and political acumen, and three men who served their country during critical, changing, turbulent times. Jackson, Polk, and Johnson were similar yet dissimilar; they were egoistic yet realistic. There might be more men elected President from New York, Virginia, and Ohio, but with the possible exception of Jefferson of Virginia, none of the Presidents of the nineteenth century faced the challenges, were more confident, or had a greater impact than the triumvirate from Tennessee.

Bibliographical Essay

In a book without footnotes or backnotes, the author and publisher owe a note of recognition to sources used in this account of Tennessee's three Presidents. Had footnotes been in order, I would have embalmed the editors of the papers of Jackson, Polk, and Johnson, whose volumes testify to their scholarship. I would also pay my respects individually to the biographers and authors of monographs and articles whose works I read. For information about the terminal illness of Jackson and Polk, I used a tape recording of Dr. Amos Christy's lecture on "Pathology of American Presidents," September 27, 1978, in the Medical School Library, East Tennessee State University.

Mature general readers, history buffs, and senior citizens not burdened with deadlines will find the letters of the Presidents worth browsing through. Robert V. Remini's *Andrew Jackson and the Course of American Empire, 1767-1821* (New York: Harper, 1977) will edify and entertain readers old and young—even in college survey courses. Marquis James's old standby *Life of Andrew Jackson, Complete in One Volume* (New York: Garden City Publishing, 1938) while formidable in size is readable. Stanley Horn's *The Hermitage, Home of Old Hickory* (New York: Greenberg, 1950) will interest general readers who use their vacations visiting historical spots.

The best biography of Polk is Charles Grier Sellers, Jr., *James K. Polk, Jacksonian, 1795-1843* (Princeton: Princeton Univ. Press, 1957) and *James K. Polk, Continentalist, 1843-1846* (Princeton: Princeton Univ. Press, 1966). Also recommended to general readers are Odie B. Faulk and Joseph A. Stout, Jr. (eds.), *The Mexican War, Changing Interpretations* (Chicago: Swallow Press, 1973); Normal A. Graebner, *Empire on the Pacific, A Study in American Continental Expansion* (New York: Ronald Press, 1955); and Frederick Merk, *Manifest Destiny and Mission in American History* (New York: Vintage Books, 1963).

Among the more moderate accounts of Johnson's confrontation with the Radicals, general readers may consult David Miller DeWitt, *The Impeachment and Trial of Andrew Johnson* (1903; rpt. New York: Russell and Russell, 1967); Eric L. McKitrick, *Andrew Johnson and Reconstruction* (Chicago: Univ. of Chicago Press, 1966); Eric L. McKitrick (ed.), *Andrew Johnson, A Profile* (New York: Hill and Wang, 1969); and Hans L. Trefousse, *Impeachment of a President: Andrew Johnson, the Blacks, and Reconstruction* (Knoxville: Univ. of Tennessee Press, 1975). See also Michael Les Benedict, *The Impeachment and Trial of Andrew Johnson* (New York: Norton, 1973); James E. Sefton, *Andrew Johnson and the Uses of Constitutional Power* (Boston: Little, Brown, 1980); and Albert Castel, *The Presidency of Andrew Johnson* (Lawrence, Kan.: Regents Press of Kansas, 1979).

Index

Other Tennessee Three Star Books

Visions of Utopia
Nashoba, Rugby, Ruskin, and the "New Communities"
    in Tennessee's Past
by John Egerton

Our Restless Earth
The Geologic Regions of Tennessee
by Edward T. Luther

Tennessee Strings
The Story of Country Music in Tennessee
by Charles K. Wolfe

Paths of the Past
Tennessee, 1770–1970
by Paul H. Bergeron

Civil War Tennessee
Battles and Leaders
by Thomas L. Connelly

Tennessee's Indian Peoples
From White Contact to Removal, 1540–1840
by Ronald N. Satz

Religion in Tennessee 1777–1945
by Herman A. Norton

Blacks in Tennessee 1791–1970
by Lester C. Lamon

Tennessee Writers
by Thomas Daniel Young

THE UNIVERSITY OF TENNESSEE PRESS : KNOXVILLE